The Speculative Remark

Cultural Memory

in

the

Present

Mieke Bal and Hent de Vries, Editors

The Speculative Remark
(One of Hegel's Bons Mots)

JEAN-LUC NANCY

Translated by Céline Surprenant

Stanford University Press
Stanford, California

Stanford University Press
Stanford, California
© 2001 by the Board of Trustees of the
Leland Stanford Junior University

Printed in the United States of America
on acid-free, archival-quality paper

Library of Congress Cataloging-in-Publication Data
Nancy, Jean-Luc.
    [Remarque spéculative. English]
    The speculative remark : one of Hegel's bons mots
    / Jean-Luc Nancy ; translated by Céline
    Surprenant.
        p.   cm.—(Cultural memory in the present)
    Includes bibliographical references and index.
    ISBN 0-8047-3713-4 (alk. paper) —
    ISBN 0-8047-3714-2 (pbk. : alk. paper)
        1. Hegel, Georg Wilhelm Friedrich, 1770–1831.
    I. Title.   II. Series.
    B2948 .N3313   2001
    193—dc21   2001020608

Original printing 2001

Last figure below indicates year of this printing:
10   09   08   07   06   05   04   03   02   01

Assistance for the translation was provided by the
French Ministry of Culture.

The Speculative Remark: (One of Hegel's Bons Mots)
was originally published in French in 1973 under the
title *La remarque spéculative: (Un bon mot de Hegel)*
© 1973, Éditions Galilée.

Typeset by BookMatters in 11/14.5 Garamond

Contents

"Speaking in Water"
by Céline Surprenant

> Here is how the text of the *Aufheben* reads: in a
> metrical, mechanical way, right at the level of its
> form, in a neutral voice, by speaking in water.
> —Jean-Luc Nancy, *The Speculative Remark*

I.

The translation of *The Speculative Remark* poses a number of technical difficulties, some of which should be pointed out:

In the original text all passages from Hegel are quoted in French,
even if, in some instances, references to the German edition alone
are given. Nancy, however, abundantly inserts either complete sentences, phrases, or words in German in all of them, and his commentary, in aiming to adhere to the terms of Hegel's text, makes
this gloss indispensable. However, some German phrases or words
to which Nancy attracts notice in the French passages do not appear in the English translation of Hegel. I have accordingly
modified the English translation following Nancy's gloss and commentary on the text when necessary. Where this would have required too drastic a retranslation of Hegel, I have simply pointed

out the absence of the terms and the transformation it imparts to Nancy's text.

This problem is in fact only one among others brought about by the unavoidable discrepancies between the French and the English translations of Hegel, imputable to the necessarily divergent relation of French and English to German but whose imprint on the translated text is everywhere apparent. The numerous instances of such disparities have unequally unsettling effects on the legibility of the book. Leaving aside for the moment the word and the concept of *Aufhebung*, one of the most visible cases is perhaps also the one that has had the most resonance as far as Nancy's work is concerned, namely, the expression *à même*, which refers, in Nancy's inflection of this idiom, to the relation that is indicated by the Hegelian *an sich*, usually translated as *in itself*; more precisely, it refers to the *nearness and separatedness* that attach to the preposition *an*. *À même* is found in Nancy's early work up until the more recent study on Hegel.[1] In *Le discours de la syncope: I. Logodaedalus* (1976), for example, Nancy speaks of the impossibility of ignoring existing interpretations when approaching Kant, writing that they are "inscribed right at the level of Kant's text" [*à même le texte de Kant*]; and later, in *Une pensée finie* (1990), Nancy points out that decision in Heidegger, taken as an exposition on the "undecidability of meaning that existence *is* . . . [,] can take place only . . . *just at* 'the impossibility of deciding.'"[2] It occurs in *Hegel, L'inquiétude du négatif* (1997), whereby to speak the language of thought "is not to speak yet another mysterious language. But it is not either, especially not, to enter into the ineffable. It is *to think*: that is, to speak right at the level of language [*à même la langue*]."[3] In *The Speculative Remark* the expression passes almost unnoticed when it first appears in the preamble (". . . all theory . . . which can be verified right at the level of Hegel's text [*à même le texte de Hegel*]"), and it will be used many times before the emphasis of the preposition *an* of the Hegelian *an sich* inflects the previous and subsequent "à même" of the book and beyond it (*RS*, 110–15). Given its pervasiveness, the idiom could serve as a guiding thread through Nancy's work, and *The Speculative Remark*, in dealing explicitly with the expression, and in drawing out its Hegelian provenance, would be our point of reference. But this might amount to nominalizing the expression, whereas what *The Speculative Remark* in fact inaugurates, and what is developed more manifestly in later works, is the opening of philosophical concepts "onto that which in natural and technical languages cannot pretend to the status of name, that is, cannot claim the status of autonomous units of sense—through the opening onto prepositions, particles and syncategoremata of all kinds," as Werner Hamacher has pointedly stated.[4] Such alteration of philosophical language cannot but have repercussions on translation. Explanatory notes in translations and commentaries of Nancy's work where *à même* appears suggest unanimously that no conjunction in English can adequately convey the relation of which Nancy writes.[5] Departing somewhat from existing translations, where *à même* is most frequently translated as "right on," "right at," or "just at," it has in most cases been translated here, perhaps more prosaically, as "right at the level"—such as in "right at the level of the text," "right at the level of form," "right at the level of grammar," and so forth. The brutal and contrasting "at the level" can remind us that if what is at issue is a relation and a formula that one could think untranslatable (as *The Speculative Remark* states with respect to the passage from German into French [*RS*, 110]), it is nevertheless not simply unutterable [*inénonçable*].[6]

The Speculative Remark discreetly gestures toward a tradition, not exclusively French, of pronouncements concerning the impenetrability of Hegel's language, which the reference to Alexandre Koyré's "Note sur la langue et la terminologie hégéliennes" signals. But even if partially to this end the book presents itself as a commentary, the terms, the language of the book, are not uniformly Hegelian. The reader will indeed soon note how Nancy plays on the proximity of Hegelian language to "ordinary language," even while such an articulation, which is precisely at issue in Hegel, runs noisily through the commentary. I have adopted as far as possible existing English translations of Hegelian terms, except where the confusion between Hegelian and "ordinary" languages is purposely aggravated.[7]

One of the exacting rules of translation whereby one should "translate the same into the same, and the different into the different" has therefore been broken.[8] The French equivalent of the Hegelian concept of *übergehen* (*passer* [to pass over]) and the series of neighboring expressions, such as the reflexive form of the verb *se passer* (to occur), are notable examples of expressions that had to be translated into a variety of verb phrases such as, among others, to pass through, to go through, to occur, to happen. Although it relates apparently less directly to the German *merken* (*RS*, 67), *remarquer*, to which diverse verbal constructions more or less closely connected to the etymology of *remarquer* (to mark again) are attached, has also been conveyed by different verbs: to draw attention to, to note, to notice, to point out. This of course applies even more to *relève*, which Jacques Derrida proposed as an equivalent of *Aufhebung* (sublation) in "The Pit and the Pyramid," and to its equivocal cognates *se relever*, *relever de*, *relevant*. Ultimately, we could include in the list of terms that oblige us to produce more than one equivalent a great number of expressions and words— such as, for example, *relief* (remnant and relief), *mettre en relief* (to bring into relief), *aller de soi* (to go without saying), *articuler* (to utter and to articulate), *retour* (return and recurrence)—that do not belong strictly to what is compiled in glossaries under the heading of Hegelian language but that, as the commentary unfolds, no longer simply stand outside of it. I have tried as far as possible to respect the lexical coherence of the text, but some of the nuances, which the ambiguous status of these terms entails, are necessarily lost in translation, a loss for which no amount of notes can make good. Further, the German word *Witz* has not been translated as "joke," "wit," or "witticism," thus following the original text and previous translations of Nancy's work on the *Witz*.[9]

Finally, anyone comparing the two versions of the text will note that many parenthetical clauses and some sentences of the original are suppressed and that some appear to have been modified more markedly than others. Jean-Luc Nancy has sanctioned these modifications and has in fact, although in rare instances, himself reformulated passages of the original.

2.

Never is the attempt to separate "technical" concerns from the philosophical import of the book more likely to fail than when dealing with *The Speculative Remark*, for the places where the translation most threatens to have an obscuring effect correspond precisely to the most salient points of the commentary. In other words, what the translation cannot help but handle roughly are the very motifs that give the commentary its movement: *relève, remarque, passer, aller de soi, à même, accent, relief.* It is as though the more these motifs refuse to be translated, the more the analyses of speculative dialectics developed in *The Speculative Remark* are confirmed.

Translation, or in any case the difference between languages, is momentarily at issue in Hegel, as Nancy points out, but it participates in a general concern for language inherent to the very object of study. Is the fundamental concept of the dialectical process, the *Aufheben*, indeed not above all well known for the "double meaning" of its word and the reflection upon language that, in Hegel's steps, it compels one to undertake? More decisively, is Hegel not the one who has insisted on the identity of being and thought, warning against isolating the difficulties of philosophical discourse (of discursivity) from the difficulties of being?[10]

Nancy's early "Essay on the Hegelian Concept of the *Aufhebung*" endorses this thought unreservedly by taking seriously the discursive problems attached to the position of the concept of the *Aufhebung* and their uneasy articulation with Hegel's so-called theory of language and of philosophical exposition (philosophical *Darstellung*). The Remark on the expression *Aufheben* of the *Science of Logic*, and its partial repetition in Hegel's other writings, provides the impulse for such an inquiry by drawing attention to the contingent speculative resources of the word *Aufheben*. As soon, however, as what might have been considered the isolated property of a fundamental concept can be extended to many other concepts, the seemingly marginal worry about the relation between a concept and its word obliges one to ask about the fate the dialectical process reserves for elements of discourse beyond words, such as the proposition, syntax, and grammar. And the commentary can all the more apply itself to reconstituting Hegel's speculative syntax and grammar, since they are not thematized as such by Hegel.

Dealing with speculative dialectics and the concept of the *Aufhebung* from the point of view of words, accent, proposition, syntax, and grammar is justified by the rules of reading philosophical writings stated in the Preface to the *Phenomenology of Spirit*. There is no question here of expounding, as the book does, on the prescriptions attached to speculative exposition. Suffice it to say that it is the impasses to which they give rise and their exacting character as far as reading is concerned that propel the study. Now if, in the Preface to the *Phenomenology*, Hegel enunciates an imperative to read philosophical propositions *otherwise* and thus makes us inherit the task of conceiving of *another* word, *another* expression, *another* grammar, *another* syntax, *another* writing, *another* style, *another* language, *another* form, this imperative reaches, for Nancy, the reading of Hegel himself. Hence the question "What is it to read Hegel?" must be asked from the outset, and it also obliges us to conceive of *another* expression, *another* grammar, and so forth. This apparently straightforward question, however, introduces not only the classical problems of presupposition and of the hermeneutic circle, which will be acute throughout the commentary, but also, as a note specifies with respect to the question now slightly displaced, an *alterity* in Hegel that one ought to try to *read*.[11]

It would not be an exaggeration to say that the intelligence of *The Speculative Remark* hangs, to a great extent, upon how one understands "alterity in Hegel," which does not necessarily only mean alterity according to Hegel. (The study asks: "Might Hegelian mastery, the *sublation* [relève] [*Aufhebung*] of the negative, not be absolutely ineluctable?" [Chapter 1].) Depending on whether one conceives of it as an absence or as an excess of determinations, or even as such an alternative, one may be tempted to assimilate it to any of the so-called motifs of the commentary, including, above all, to the *Aufheben*. Hence, supposing that it be indistinguishable from the movement of sublation as the book describes it, the "alterity in Hegel" might be thought to take the form of a disappearing, to consist in a "negative epiphany":[12] sublation "resists any effort to explain it" (*RS*, 152), "refuses to let itself be identified" (57), takes place as a "pure metrics" (127); its syntax is a *Zerstören*, a destruction (127), and it is graspable only by letting it vanish (109). From this view Nancy's "negotiations" with Hegel's texts would serve the purpose of marking the places of such vanishings.[13] But nothing would be as misleading as such an accentuation of vanishing alone. One must also note how the process of sublation is characterized by an excess of occurrences ("it repeatedly occurs," as we will read), which the commentary no less registers.

Instead of going through it in order to discern in each of its moments what kind of "alterity" is at issue—*The Speculative Remark* does not allow for dealing with "alterity" in this way—let us briefly and finally consider what, at various moments, is called *Hegel's text*, for the weight of the demonstration lies to a large extent on it. If it is no more *easily locatable* than "alterity," it does appear to encompass all the displacements, the slidings, the gaps, the floating, the vanishing, whose repercussions the commentary underlines whenever the *aufheben* and the *language* of speculative dialectics are at issue. From this view the *text* might be the unique *figure* of alterity that one "ought to try to read," in which case our perplexities over the mode of presence of the *text* might turn out to redouble those that the commentary discerns in Hegel around the mode of presentation of the transient concept. Hence that *The Speculative Remark* should demonstrate how "dialectics functions only through decisions taken elsewhere," as Nancy writes in a subsequent work, has a special resonance here, since the question arises as to what sort of "other place," if any, the text might stand for (should "another place" be added to the list of modifications prescribed by speculative dialectics?).[14]

"Reading otherwise," then, engages the various forms of blockage of speculative dialectics that *Hegel's text* presents, such as, for example, the neutralization of the voice, mechanical recitation, the "singular literality" of certain metaphors, the warding off of the dangers of the *Witz*. But here, too, it is never simply a matter of seizing points of resistance to speculative dialectics, forms of subtractions from it. The unsettlement, the slidings, the "accumulation of gaps" to which the text points, as so many instances of such halting, cannot be the prerogative of any isolated moment, however disruptive, and ought rather permanently to be thought of as an incessant movement, an unrest. We might be tempted to identify the *aufheben* with this "movement," in which case *The Speculative Remark* replies that the latter rather precisely troubles the conceptual identity of the *aufheben* (*RS*, 109). At least one mode of presence of the *text* as the alterity "one ought to try to read" might therefore be a continuous reminder to us of the conceit of aiming to dissipate this movement, whether it be by arresting it or by apprehending it as a disappearing.

For that reason, in addition to reading *The Speculative Remark* in relation to the recent work on Hegel, it might be useful to refer to some of the author's works more or less contemporary, and not just chronologically, with our text. Nancy makes many signs throughout these texts toward the *apprehension* of the undecidable, just as, in the vein of Derrida's work, and as we briefly indicated, it is one of the stakes of his reading of Hegel. In *Ego Sum* Nancy speaks of the "undecidable taken as such"—mutatis mutandis, the attempt to arrest the movement of the text—as the most acute way in which a discourse "gives itself the consistence, the substance and the stature of subject."[15] In the preamble to *Le discours de la syncope: I. Logodaedalus*, more particularly in its polemical development on the effects of fashion (on *la mode* and *le mode*), Nancy even goes so far as to speak of "the transubstantiation, in a hitherto unheard sense, of everything [including the thought of the undecidable] which . . . cuts into and undoes the system of substance" whereby everything that displaces this system is hypostatized (7).

We cannot here examine in detail how the preoccupation with the substance and with the subject from the point of view of "the undecidable taken as such" can be articulated with Hegel's undecidable discourse of the *Aufhebung*, as the book invites us to do. Suffice it to say that although *The Speculative Remark* is unmistakably concerned with the *text* (with *Hegel's* text), the concept of the text that might be said to emerge from it cannot hastily be assimilated to all other works and thought where issues of text and reading stand out.[16] Such a problematics signals an ongoing concern for the inheritance of romanticism as it emerges in filigree in *The Speculative Remark* and explicitly in Nancy's work on the concept of Literature and on the *Witz*.[17] But even if such a concern finds a unique formulation in his work, the preoccupation with textuality is not explainable only with respect to it. Incidentally, one of Nancy's rare direct statements on the "problematics of textuality" is found in a preface written not long after *The Speculative Remark* for a book devoted to textual invention in Kant. The passage deserves to be quoted at length or perhaps even *annexed* to the book:

Somewhere . . . in a place and time which cannot be assigned by the discourse of philosophy, something trembles or vacillates, something collapses in the very movement of foundation, something which inaugurates philosophy occurs in a sort of jolt, of throb or of pulsation—perhaps also a drive [*pulsion*], as at the confines where Freud has ventured, an indissociable life (and) death drive. And it is precisely what is at issue in problematics of textuality. The latter are in this way problematics in the plural, for there is no system, no order, no monological field which confers upon them the unity of a discourse; but they are problematics, in the most rigorous sense of the word . . . at the same time as their very rigor makes of them, in the strongest but not the most pathetic sense, unrests [*inquiétudes*].[18]

Abbreviations

The following abbreviations have been used in the text for frequently cited works by Hegel:

A   *Aesthetics: Lectures on Fine Art.* 2 vols. Trans. T. M. Knox. Oxford: Clarendon Press, 1975. [*Aesthetik.* Frankfurt am Main: Suhrkamp, 1970.]

Enc. I   *The Encyclopedia Logic (with the Zusätze).* Trans. T. F. Geraets, W. A. Suchting, and H. S. Harris. Indianapolis: Hackett, 1991. [*Die Wissenschaft der Logik. Erster Teil. Enzyklopädie der Philosophischen Wissenschaften im Grundrisse, 1830.* Hamburg: F. Meiner, 1992.]

Enc. II *Philosophy of Nature: Being Part Two of the Encyclopedia of the Philosophical Sciences (1830).* Trans. A. V. Miller. Oxford: Clarendon Press, 1970. [*Naturphilosophie. Zweiter Teil. Enzyklopädie der Philosophischen Wissenschaften im Grundrisse, 1830.* Hamburg: F. Meiner, 1992.]

Enc. III *Philosophy of Mind: Being Part Three of the Encyclopedia of the Philosophical Sciences (1830).* Trans. W. Wallace, together with the Zusätze in Boumann's text (1845), trans. A. V. Miller. Oxford: Clarendon Press, 1971. [*Philosophie des Geistes. Dritter Teil. Enzyklopädie*

der Philosophischen Wissenschaften im Grundrisse, 1830.
Hamburg: F. Meiner, 1992.]

LHP   *Lectures on the History of Philosophy.* 3 vols. Trans.
E. S. Haldane. Lincoln: University of Nebraska Press,
1995. [*Vorlesungen über die Geschichte der Philosophie.
Teil 2 Griechische Philosophie I: Thales bis Kyniker.*
Hamburg: F. Meiner, 1989.]

PS   *Phenomenology of Spirit.* Trans. A. V. Miller. Oxford:
Oxford University Press, 1977. [*Phänomenologie des
Geistes.* Ed. J. Hoffmeister. Hamburg: F. Meiner,
1952.]

SL   *Hegel's Science of Logic.* Trans. A. V. Miller. New York:
Humanity Books, 1969. [*Wissenschaft der Logik.* Ed.
G. Lasson. Hamburg: F. Meiner, 1971.]

And also:

RS   J.-L. Nancy. *La remarque spéculative: Un bon mot de
Hegel.* Paris: Galilée, 1973.

SE   Sigmund Freud. *The Standard Edition of the Works of
Sigmund Freud.* Trans. and ed. James Strachey.
London: Hogarth, 1953–74.

The Speculative Remark
(One of Hegel's Bons Mots)

(One does not shy away, in the title, from the risk or from the possible ridicule of "making a *Witz*"—or two, if the latter divides in two; it was perhaps here more unavoidable than anywhere else—perhaps also for the same reason more unforgivable. The possibility of a unique and strict technical wording has continually evaded us; for example: *Essay on the Hegelian Concept of Aufheben*, which is yet also the exact description of this work—and it has evaded us for reasons that will no doubt finally appear through reading. It was necessary to choose between words [one must choose the lesser of two evils, as one says],[1] unless, as has indeed happened, the choice should be left suspended between two titles that will each, in turn or together, the one through the other, attempt to "justify" themselves. But it might be useful to recall, in order to begin the reading, some other possibilities that have been neither preserved nor suppressed: thus *Eigensinn* [combination of the literal meaning (*sens*) and of the obstinate whim, such as Hegel uses][2] or *The Antithetical Meanings of Speculative Words* [close to Freud by one word], or even, if you like, it goes without saying, *Hebufena*.)

One of Hegel's Bons Mots

This is exactly Jacobi's concern: to replace philosophical Ideas with *expressions and words* which are not supposed to give knowledge or understanding. These words and expressions may well have a philosophical meaning; but Jacobi's polemic is directed precisely against the philosophies which take them seriously and make their philosophical meaning articulate.

—Hegel, *Faith and Knowledge: An English Translation of "Glauben und Wissen"*

He was right not to content himself with the formations to which this thought leads [the *Aufklärung* and Kant], and yet he makes all that fuss only so as to get his word in [*um das Wort zu sagen*]; blathering against thought and reason in general . . . he spreads or rather he bolts together remote baroque expressions and completely mystifies the reader.

—Hegel, "Hamann's Schriften"

Der *Schein* selbst ist dem *Wesen* wesentlich, die Wahrheit wäre nicht, wenn sie nicht schiene und erschiene.

—Hegel, *Aesthetik*

1

Preamble

> . . . but what thus stands on the threshold often
> for that reason is least adequate.
> —Hegel, *Logic*, §205

1. Preamble, which is also to say: "Discourse which does not get to the point." —Littré, *Dictionnaire de la langue française*

2. In this work we will take for granted—if that makes any sense—the following analyses or texts: Alexandre Koyré, "Note sur la langue et la terminologie hégéliennes";[1] Jean Hyppolite, *Logic and Existence* (first part);[2] Werner Marx, *Absolute Reflexion und Sprache*;[3] and Jacques Derrida, "From Restricted to General Economy: A Hegelianism Without Reserve" and "The Pit and the Pyramid: Introduction to Hegel's Semiology."[4]

This is to say, in more ways than one, that we will not feel obliged to go back over many well-established *theoretical truths* of Hegelianism—without these truths being absent or without, moreover, renouncing all theory (even if we cannot restrict ourselves to it), which can be verified right at the level of Hegel's text [*à même le texte de Hegel*].

3."One of Hegel's bons mots. ". . . This should be, if we began in all semantic simplicity, the title of a story or, better still, of an anecdote (which is to say, literally, of a *hitherto unpublished* story, which did not figure in Hegel's books). The genre would then be that of a philosophers' almanac,[5] the style that of a narrative [*récit*], and even then—a narrative reduced to its most tenuous (but, perhaps, its most elegant) formula, the narrator merely reporting that "one day, Hegel . . . ";[6] and we would here have to do scarcely more than to report "one of Hegel's bons mots."

It would, of course, be impossible to do so in all innocence. That is, by ignoring, for example, that the genre (or part of the genre) imposed on the *preliminary* exposition of (Hegelian) science is already the narrative, narration: "what has been said here does express the concept but cannot count for more than an anticipatory assurance. Its truth does not lie in this partly narrative exposition" (*PS*, 35). To miss or fall short of Hegelian *truth*, on the one hand, and to remain, in spite of everything, in the regime of a Hegelian preface—that is, still in spite of everything, in the regime of the concept—is the double gesture, two-speed pace to which we will be simultaneously constrained. That such a constraint, however, might be itself Hegelian, or might fall under Hegel's discourse in one way or another, is also the question or, perhaps less imprecisely, the oddness [*bizarrerie*] and, in any case, the strangeness [*étrangeté*] that should ceaselessly be stirring here.

The narrative form, then, will not exceed the title (which is in fact only partly narrative), and what the latter entitles remains first and foremost subjected to a lack of style—to the lack of a style. This is however not in order to allow this slavery to produce, through its work, its own negation and set itself up as mastery. Might Hegelian mastery, the *sublation* [relève] (*Aufhebung*) of the negative, not be absolutely ineluctable—even if no discourse, as such, can withdraw from it—such is henceforth the chance that must be taken. *The chance of finding, by surprise, chance in Hegel:*

this is what we should try to say, and to say precisely, about the mainspring of mastery, that is, about the *sublation* of the negative. This is why the *Aufhebung* is the object of this "work."

It is difficult to see, no doubt, how the term and the theme of the *Aufhebung* could be taken from Hegel and isolated for the purpose of a particular examination. Admittedly, it goes without saying that this "object" can be constituted as an object only on the—overwhelming . . . —condition that it encompass not what is elsewhere called its ins and outs, its corollaries and its implications, but rather Hegelian systematicity itself, in the totality of its constituency, through the exhaustive course of its steps and articulations. And in a certain way it equally goes without saying that no one can undertake less (insofar as one wishes to *produce* a *discourse*—in the rigorous sense of the word) than a preface (or a postface) to the total reading of Hegel. Yet again, this is a matter of slavery, if Hegel indeed holds the mastery of discourse—a matter of slavery, and not of ambition (assuming that it does not amount to the same thing). Undertaking to work the *Aufhebung*, or to work on the *Aufhebung*,[7] would thus be—all narration this time definitively excluded—nothing but undertaking to draw the program of a general (and perhaps absolute) commentary on Hegel. One should not shy away from this task because of its size: if dimensions and, in any case, the *general* character of such a commentary are at issue, it is only a matter of time, and of a patience whose secret a certain academic genre possesses (which is probably not exactly the patience of the Hegelian concept).

> (*An empirical limit might not be a limit: it might suffice to say: "Hegel must be commented upon by all, not by one."*)

And one might thus discover that it is all the less possible to shy away from this task, that one is already caught within it, that one has already commented on Hegel, that one has never been doing anything else, under the heading of what is called and is determined as *philosophy*, than to comment on Hegel.

But it is rather the task itself that risks evading us—with respect, this time, to the *absolute* character of the commentary. If it is (in a Hegelian manner) indeed true that generality, here, must become absoluteness [*absoluité*], must be *sublated* into the absolute, on the one hand, and if, on the other, commenting on is first and foremost just simply reading, but reading with precision, exhaustively, truly reading, and, therefore, reading absolutely—what is it then to read Hegel? Whatever we aim to do, or not to do, with this or that Hegelian concept (for example, the *Aufhebung*), we have to go through this first.

What is it to read Hegel?

To this question, brought to light as a necessary preamble to the Hegelian progress, Hegel himself cannot, in the absolute (that is, as a discourse of the absolute), fail to answer. Indeed he does not fail on this point. This does not mean that he delivers the key to the reading at issue. The text of his answer is well known:

Here we see the reason [*Grund*] behind one particular complaint so often made against them: that so much has to be read over and over [*wiederholt gelesen werden*] before it can be understood—a complaint whose burden is presumed to be quite outrageous and final,[8] and, if justified [*gegründet*], to admit of no defence [*Gegenrede*]. It is clear from the above what this amounts to. The philosophical proposition [*Satz*], since it *is* a proposition, leads one to believe [*Meinung*] that the usual subject-predicate relation obtains, as well as the usual attitude towards knowing. But the philosophical content destroys this attitude and this opinion. We learn by experience that we meant something other than we meant to mean; and this correction of our meaning compels our knowing to go back to the proposition, and understand [*fassen*] it in some other way. . . .

The one method interferes with the other, and only a philosophical exposition [*Exposition*] that rigidly excludes the usual way of relating the parts of a proposition could achieve the goal of plasticity [*plastisch*]. . . .

The sublation of the form [*Form*] of the proposition must not happen only in an *immediate* manner, through the mere content of the proposition. On the contrary, this opposite movement must find explicit expression [*ausgesprochen*]; . . . This alone is the speculative *in act* [das *wirkliche* Speculative], and only the expression of this movement is a speculative exposition [*Darstellung*]. (*PS*, 39–40)

There is no question of commenting on this text as yet, with all that it presupposes:[9] it is the latter that prescribes the commentary and the reading of Hegel. And even if it means that we later discover ourselves to be doomed (or that we have doomed ourselves, insofar as we were aiming to read Hegel), to reread this text, perhaps to reread no other text than this one, we must still begin by remembering its rule (one would like to say, as one does for the purpose of beginning: at least its formal rule—but it is readily apparent how delicate the handling of such a distinction becomes in this text): the understanding [*compréhension*] of philosophical writing is first of all signaled by a defect; its reading must be repeated. How many times? We are not told; the question is irrelevant—from the outset, this repetition escapes measurement. Consequently, the reproach commonly leveled at this defect is "outrageous [*ungebührtig*] and final," and the philosophical book thus finds itself, at least seemingly, peremptorily disqualified. Now, if Hegel's text comes to "clarify the matter," it is not in order to reply to the reproach, in order to hold forth a *Gegenrede*, a contrary discourse against it (and therefore on its ground). For, in accordance with the text, it is precisely insofar as the reproach formulated in this way finds its *Grund* (its reason and its ground) that it admits of no refutation—and as we saw, it is this *Grund* that is here uncovered in the text. Through the singular logic of a reply that does not answer, Hegel has already subtracted his text from the logic of argumentation, from the play of the *Gegenreden*, of discourses of opposition, and perhaps, from the play of the *Rede*, of discourse as such and in general.

Hegel answers:[10] the repetition of reading is indeed necessary; it is the return of knowledge to the proposition, the philosophical content of which has disappointed or dislodged opinion (the *Meinung*, the thought that is *mine* alone). The reproach is thus justified by what impugns it. In other words—one must no doubt point this out [*le remarquer*], and in a certain sense, this is all there is to point out here—this reproach, qua reproach, was, still or already, itself a proposition to which one simply nods assent and to which knowledge here returns or, better, over which the reader, if he has been the reader of the philosophical content of this preface, must already have returned. The genuine reader has *already reread*.

In spite of the particular manner of this "argumentation," there would be nothing here that was not quite banal if the text did not determine more precisely the mode of this repetition, of this rereading. It could indeed be simply a matter of a "more profound comprehension," of a "better understanding" [*intelligence*] of philosophical writing. That, however, is not what Hegel writes here. It is a question of *grasping—fassen*—the proposition otherwise, insofar as it is a philosophical proposition; it is therefore not a question, at least not expressly, of understanding it—*verstehen*—nor of conceiving it—*begreifen*. *Fassen* (to seize, to contain and to hold; *Fass*, the barrel) may well be commonly taken as a metaphor, or as a catachresis, of one term or the other. But it is no doubt difficult to leave it at that—at the metaphor of an undifferentiated "understanding"—when we know the difference between the thought and the concept of understanding [*entendement*] to which Hegel everywhere appeals and, furthermore, when one learns about the use Hegel can make of the proper and the figural meaning [*sens*] of so many words (this is what we want to learn here; we must not, as far as possible, therefore anticipate . . .). *Fassen* is to grasp, to catch, to take something in hand [*prendre en main*]. It is a matter of grasping [*empoigner*] the proposition otherwise—and of grasping the entire philosophical writing by another end, by two ends, or still otherwise, who knows? It is, in any case, not only a matter of the meaning of this proposition but rather of its form.

All this is clearly not blindly guessed by using the word *fassen*—a use that, after all, is itself *also* accidental and accessory, even though it recurs in more than one comparable instance in Hegel. It is rather the rest of the text that will have allowed us to understand [*entendre*] (to grasp?) this word. As we read, Hegel's answer indeed soon and rigorously unfolds as a reflection on the constitution of the proposition. The antagonism between opinion and knowledge, which makes the rereading compulsory, must be resolved through an exclusion of "the usual way of relating the parts of a proposition." Nothing less, consequently, than the program (still to be accomplished) of another—absolutely other—grammar. Hence, it is no longer only a question of reading or rereading. On the contrary, Hegel's reader finds himself—and yet again through a singular movement, which is in any case not set out in itself—transported to the writing (let us first say, in all rigor and simplicity: to the composition) of the philosophical text—to its *exposition*: the repetition of reading is now assigned to the latter, which becomes the *plasticity* of the exposition. *Plasticity* is therefore the exclusion (the prohibition? the disruption? the mutation? the transmutation?) of the usual relation between the parts of discourse—the other grammar. To read Hegel's text is thus, if not to rewrite it, at least to repeat its exposition *plastically*.[11]

It remains to be verified whether this "rule" really conforms to the determinations the text has seemingly successively produced. Hegel does it himself by going on to write: the philosophical *fassen* is concerned with the *form* of the proposition, and can in no way be confined to an understanding [*intelligence*] of the content (or else: the status of content does not contain the philosophical content, which involves form, the *fassen* of form). The opposition of knowledge to *meinen* and the return of the one to the other must be "expressed"—and this, not in accordance with secondary communicative or commercial requirements (the proof that "the reader" who, through his reproach, has launched this demonstration, does not fall under any of these headings) but rather in the name of an intrinsic necessity, for only an "expression" (*aussprechen*: to speak out, to state) can allow the reading of an exposition; that is, only an "expression" can constitute an exposition. But the speculative "expression" is the one that will be offered to the reader (and to the scriptor), this time, as a *presentation* (*Darstellung*). The *Darstellung* is not, as we know, the accessory instrumental element or event of a performance or of a publication (for example); it is itself the actuality [*effectivité*] of the presence and of the present of the speculative—of a speculative that is what it is only insofar as it presents the present (and therefore only insofar as it presents itself). To speak here, as one at times and too often does, of a perfectly adequate and transparent expression, or of the epiphany of the speculative absolute, is still rather insufficient if not seriously erroneous: such formulas still enclose the relative exteriority of a milieu of manifestation, however pure this milieu may be. The speculative is rather itself its own milieu of manifestation; it has *in itself* the being-middle of the middle [*il a* en lui *l'être-milieu du milieu*],[12] and its presence is actualized—and is actualized only—*as* its presentation.[13] This actualization, however, is not without consequences and perhaps not without some complications, with which the reading will precisely not fail to confront us. For the moment let us remember the "figure" that this reading, this writing takes: the *fassen* of presence that presents itself, as it presents itself; here, now, in the middle of the page, a piece of writing presents itself to its reader; a presence writes itself and is read—right at the level of the text [*à même le texte*].

The presentation determined in this way, however, depends on—*as we read*—a specific operation: the form of the proposition must be *aufgehoben*, sublated. We can at least read this much about this operation of sublation: the sublation of form could not take place "through the mere content of the proposition." The sublation of form therefore at least also takes place thanks to its form and precisely in form itself. How, then, must one describe this operation? How must it be *conceived* and, altogether, somehow *formalized*?

We see that here, now, the ground is suddenly giving way under our feet. The reading of Hegel is forced on whoever wants to decipher something of the *Aufhebung*—but the *Aufhebung* is already prescribed to whoever wants to read Hegel. To read—effectively and speculatively—is to have already sublated Hegel's (propositions) text, or rather, it is identically and presently to sublate it. *Plasticity*—the product of the *Aufhebung*—precedes its own production, exactly as (and because) the repetition of reading precedes the reading of presentation, of this sublated presentation where the speculative (will be) is presented (given).

There is nothing surprising about this circle, no doubt, and this entire preamble—which indeed does not get to the "point" . . . because it is already there, and loses itself on it—brings us back to a hermeneutical constraint that may control any philosophical reading (and, reciprocally, any philosophical model or philosophy of reading in general, whether it be a question of understanding a text, of interpreting it, of criticizing it, of meditating on it, or indeed, as we shall see, of learning it by heart). In order to be read, any philosophy has, as such, always required the presupposition of its concept.[14] Hegelian reading submits to this request—and submits to it, more precisely, by appealing, in its presentation of the philosophical book, to philosophical reading or writing (and, let us note in passing, the latter already constitutes for Hegel a tradition of the epoch of the philosophical book). That the *Aufhebung* be legible only through the *Aufhebung* first and foremost simply means that it is a philosophical concept and that, as such, it must be grasped philosophically (the *fassen*). To read philosophy, and to read, as we say, philosophically, such is also the broadest constituency where a program of work on one of Hegel's bons mots is drawn. . . .

One must nevertheless have begun to suspect that the figure or the model that Hegelian reading constitutes in relation to philosophical reading in general repeats or accomplishes, at least in a singular mode, the hermeneutic circle that is characteristic of it (a mode that is nevertheless linked systematically with the particular status Hegel aims to give to his Preface, to this "partly narrative exposition," which must not be a "preliminary clarification"). Indeed, not only is no precondition here laid down—nothing is provisionally required of the reader's belief or of his trust, no special aptitude is expected of him—but, more generally, the hermeneutical regime, insofar as it is one of a necessary *presupposition*, merges with the regime of a *positing* [position]. Repeated, the circle is dislodged, out of line. For, to the extent (and this is to the full extent) that reading—exposition in general—must obey the rule of the sublated and the sublating *plasticity* of propositions (in their content *and their form*), this plasticity, as such, does not *present* itself anywhere else than in Hegel's text, in the text that we are reading, here, now (but *in* here does precisely not mean "inside" nor "in the spirit" of the text). Hegelian hermeneutic, the hermeneutic of the *fassen*, is given right at the level of the text, and nothing precedes (nor exceeds?) this text. Just as there is no preface, there is no pre-positing [*pre-position*] to Hegelianism [*il n'y a pas de pré-posé au hégélianisme*].[15] No doubt the *Aufhebung* is presupposed, but the presupposition of the *Aufhebung* is (to be read in) the positing of the *Aufhebung*, is in some way the very presence of the text. To read Hegel, then, is simply, if one dare say so, to read Hegel—or even: the *Aufhebung*, the sublation necessary to reading, takes place in the text that we are reading.

Yet for the second time the ground is giving way under our

feet—albeit in a different manner: it is no longer an abyss that opens it up but a fissure that tears it, the borders of which are uncertain, and that goes we know not how far. For at the very moment—in the text itself—that Hegel offers us the philosophical writing to read openly and, so to speak, in its literality, he takes away, or at least dislodges, this very literality. And this for two reasons: if, first, the *Aufhebung* of the propositional form is necessary, it is because the proposition, through its mere grammatical disposition, "leads one to believe that the usual subject-predicate relation obtains"; now, philosophical writing is composed of philosophical propositions, which are precisely propositions, that is, ordinary propositions submitted to the grammar of their usual relation. If, on the other hand, the plasticity of the exposition is to be achieved in the very form of the proposition, we will have noticed how, without further clarifications, Hegel invokes this plasticity by means of the conditional and the modality of the must ("the sublation of the form of the proposition must not happen only . . .").[16] In these two ways, then—which indeed constitute a single gesture—Hegel takes away the sublated literality that must be read— that we should henceforth read. But where, toward what is it sent? This is what is not written. On the one hand, philosophy writes or is written in ordinary propositions, and in these propositions it writes about the sublation of the "usual subject-predicate relation"; on the other hand—the conditional or the having-to-be—the "rigorous exclusion" of this relation announces, if it does not state it, *another* genre of propositions, *another* grammar or grammaticality. Between the two, something indeed appears to be missing, and what is missing in this way, what else can it be but the *Aufhebung*? The *Aufhebung* is thus taken away—at least displaced, or posted out of line, and sublation *does not quite take place*—at the very point where its presence appeared to be inscribed and, especially, at the very point where, in all necessity, this inscription was required if only for reading to be allowed to begin.

But after all, we have nevertheless already started to read; we have already started to read the *Aufhebung* in the text. . . . This thoroughly empirical observation, whose irony now looms before us, turns out to repeat the rule of reading that we believed we had received from Hegel (to read him is to read his text . . .) and that we have immediately lost. We know where this lost rule hides itself: it is in the text; but we do not know how to discover its hiding place, since we lack the rule, the plasticity of the text, through which the *Darstellung* is possible. Everything begins with this imbroglio, and everything could very well end with it. If we want to pull through, we must—à la commedia dell'arte—improvise, and without knowing our lines we must make progress through the plot. (We will come back later to the roles that we could have learned by heart—as well as to the stage or the stages where we could have played).

We can in any case continue reading Hegel. We cannot, however, confine ourselves—we cannot hold on to—the propositions of his discourse nor to the grammar of their ordinary relations. Grammatical and logical assurance *ought to* fail us; it will be dispersed by reading, by the repetition of reading, in this writing of sorts, where Hegel's *exposition* carries us, sublating the ordinary rigor of its statements [*énoncés*]. Hegel says it: "What is asserted to be a fixed Law that is in itself constant can only be a moment of the unity which is reflected into itself, can only appear as a vanishing magnitude" (*PS*, 181).

Yet what will we be reading other than Hegel's statements (the propositions)? But if we have to read them as *moments*, what is a *moment*, and what is a "vanishing magnitude"? It is, as we will learn (that is, reread), nothing that can be separated from the *Aufhebung*. What will we be reading other than the *Aufhebung*?—We will therefore read haltingly and thus remain, for as long as it takes, in an "exposition that has a narrative character." Between two genres, we lack a style; a pen (to which we will have to return at the end) escapes us, the style and the pen of the *Aufhebung*. This preamble will thus have been a complete waste of time.

Dispossessed or unsettled in this manner, we will be reading, or be writing, nothing else but the gap [*écart*], the displacement that produces this disruption in Hegel's text—or, if you like, this alteration in the course of which the necessity of another grammar, of another proposition, is being proposed. We must, without any further warnings, since the entire system of warnings has just revealed itself to be useless, read these *others*, or this *other*, in Hegel, which is to say, of course, read Hegel *otherwise*, and finally, to come (back) to our "object," read or write *otherwise* the *Aufhebung*. (No doubt, we will simultaneously note that the absence of warning, of which we just spoke, has nothing to do with the impulsive or furious decision to submit Hegel to the arbitrariness of an interpretation or a use.)[17]

2

Of a Text to Be Marked Again

Hegel condensed the mistake; he systematized it, proffered it, so to speak, entirely, and entirely in a word. His formula is on the frontispiece of Satan's School, which henceforth scorns imitators by defying them to do better. Satan recognized himself in the Hegelian formula, admired it as one of his own; for Pride, Satan and Hegel together shout: Being and Nothing are identical.
—E. Hello, *L'homme*

This is what the word *aufgehoben*, which is fundamental in Hegel's system, expresses.
—E. Boutroux, "Sur la nécessité, la finalité et la liberté chez Hegel"

We must begin, then, by moving around Hegel's text, Hegel himself having dislodged us from what seemed as though it should be the required *incipit* or *introït* of its reading. Through this first (second) adventurous reading (whose discursive, systematic necessities the reader is at least momentarily prevented from keeping an exact record of, just as he is of the relation between parts of Hegel's discourse), in quest of the access that has been concealed from him, one text, only one, soon draws attention to itself [*se fait bien vite remarquer*]—and it does so immediately for at least two reasons. First, it deals with the *Aufhebung*; second, it is separated by an entire book from the text that we had to read in preamble, and in a certain way it is even separated from the book to which it otherwise belongs. The text in question is the Remark that the *Science of Logic* devotes to the *Aufhebung*. It is the Remark to the last sec-

tion of the first chapter of the first book. And since we are dedi-
cated to reading, let us begin by simply reading this text:

The table of contents points to it in the following manner: *Remark:
The Expression "To Sublate"* [*Anmerkung: Ausdruck: aufheben*]. But
the main text only mentions Remark, which is followed by our text
(the passages Hegel added in the second edition of the *Science of
Logic* [1831] appear in square brackets):

To sublate and the *sublated* [*das Ideelle*] (that which exists ideally as a moment) constitute one of the most important [*wichtig*] notions in philosophy. It is a fundamental determination which repeatedly occurs throughout the whole of philosophy [*die schlechthin allenthalben wiederkehrt*], the
meaning of which is to be clearly grasped and especially distinguished
from *nothing*. What is sublated is not thereby reduced to nothing [*Nichts*].
Nothing is *immediate*; what is sublated, on the other hand, is the result of
mediation; it is a nonbeing but as a *result* which had its origin in a being.
It still has, therefore, *in itself* the *determinateness* [*Bestimmtheit*] *from which
it originates.*

"To sublate" has a twofold meaning in the language: on the one hand
it means to preserve [*aufbewahren*], to *maintain* [*erhalten*], and equally it
also means to cause to cease, to put an end to [*ein Ende machen*]. Even "to
preserve" includes a negative element, namely, that something is removed
from its immediacy, and so from an existence which is open to external
influences, in order to preserve it. Thus what is sublated is at the same
time preserved [*ein zugleich Aufbewarhtes*]; it has only lost its immediacy
but is not on that account annihilated [*vernichtet*]. [The two definitions
of "to *sublate*" which we have given can be quoted as two dictionary
meanings (*Bedeutung*) of this word (*aufgeführt werden*). But it is certainly
remarkable to find that a language has come to use one and the same
word for two opposite meanings. It is a delight to speculative thought (*ist
es erfreulich*) to find in the language words which have in themselves (*an
ihnen selbst*) a speculative meaning; the German language has a number
of such. The double meaning of the Latin *tollere* (which has become famous through the Ciceronian pun [*Witz*] *tollendum esse Octavium*) does
not go so far; its affirmative determination signifies only a lifting up
(*Emporheben*).] Something is sublated only insofar as it has entered into
unity with its opposite; in this more particular signification as something reflected, it may fittingly be called a *moment* [*Moment*]. In the case

of the lever, weight and distance from a point are called its mechanical moments on account of the sameness [*Dieselbigkeit*] of their effect, in spite of the contrast [*Verschiedenheit*] otherwise between something real, such as a weight, and something ideal, such as a spatial determination, a line [see *Enc. II*, § 261, Remark]. We shall often have occasion to notice [*Bemerkung*] that the technical language [*Kunstsprache*] of philosophy employs Latin terms for reflected determinations [either because the mother tongue has no words for them or if it has, as here, because its expression calls to mind (*erinnert*) more what is immediate, whereas the foreign language suggests more what is reflected.]

The more precise meaning and expression [*der nähere Sinn und Ausdruck*] which being and nothing receive [*erhalten*], now that they are *moments*, is to be ascertained from the consideration of determinate being as the unity in which they are preserved. . . . [1]

We can here interrupt the text, which, in its few concluding lines, recapitulates briefly the preceding chapter and introduces the first determination of the object of the following one: determinate being. But we will not suspend our reading without noting that, through its last paragraph, the Remark *also* acts as a passage or a transition from one chapter to the other, more precisely, from the first to the second chapter of the *Science of Logic*. It functions, then, both as an appendix and as a moment of discourse. And having to read the note *in* the midst of the text, that is, discourse *in* what draws attention to it [*dans sa remarque*], is by no means the least of the constraints to which we will be submitted. The singular conjunction of the *passage* (that is, of the dialectical articulation or of the development [*Entwicklung*] in the Hegelian sense), and of the *annex* (what one notices or points out *in passing* [*fait remarquer*]), of the marginal or the adjacent meaning and mark might even provide the most general form of the questions around which we shall have to move. For admittedly, if it is true that this Remark belongs to the systematic economy of the *Science of Logic*, it is no less true that nothing in this economy expressly has or will come to justify and to ground its position as a remark, or as a "detached" text.[2] This is the first motif with respect to which this text draws attention to itself [*se fait remarquer*].

It is in any case what obliges us to begin by "situating" this text within the economy on which it depends—as is indeed usually required in an explication de texte. But here, following this rule is a matter of urgency because this "detached" remark appears already to have no connections with its context other than doubtful or precarious ones . . . (yet, let us be warned, this urgency will arise in the course of an interminable passage through almost the entire text that precedes the Remark. Ultimately, one will continually be getting to it, to this noticeable because also unobtainable or improbable text, up to the point where, in a few pages, one may well appear to have forgotten it. Let us be patient . . .).

First, let us note that this text does not belong to the set of paragraphs that the *Encyclopedia* devotes to language nor to any other texts where Hegel deals with language for itself. It is not part of the Hegelian theory of language or, more broadly, of Hegelian semiology insofar as they have their place in the system. But this chiefly holds for the reverse: the texts devoted to language (themselves essentially Remarks) do not pay too much attention to the twofold speculative meaning of certain words. The theory (if it is one—and, in any case, the practice) of the twofold meaning [*sens*] of *aufheben* is not articulated to the theory of meaning [*signification*]. But it is appended to the logic,[3] in a word and as we know, to the text that makes up the program and the closure of the system. That is to say, moreover, this time from an empirical point of view (but is it unrelated to the preceding one?), that it is appended to the text whose second edition Hegel prepares in 1831. Now, if, a moment ago, in the course of reading, we were able to pick out the (provisionally quantitative) importance of Hegel's additions to the second version of that Remark, let us recall that the preface written for the second edition opens with a long (and more famous) text concerning German language and its philosophical privileges. This preface is the last text that Hegel wrote: he signed it seven days before his death. The preface of the second edition of the *Science of Logic* will thus have been written out of the amplified Remark on *aufheben*. In due course we will also read the preface. But before being able to interrogate that singular proliferation of an auxiliary motif, let us consider its systematic position.

As the first sentence of the Remark indicates, this motif consists of going back over a *concept* [*Begriff*], and this avowed conceptuality of the *aufheben* constitutes one of the main features distinguishing the text of the *Science of Logic* from the analogous texts that we recalled (in notes). The Remark gives some precisions on "one of the most important concepts of philosophy"—(*wichtig*, weighty, which tips the scales)—and that "repeatedly occurs throughout the whole of philosophy"—purely and simply (*schlechthin*, one could translate: absolutely, if we were not in Hegel . . .).[4] *Throughout the whole of philosophy*: indeed, the *aufheben* has already operated in the first chapter. As expected and as its first sentence indicates, the Remark that recalls and that does not foretell comes belatedly [*vient après coup*]. How has the *aufheben*—the concept—already occurred again in the text?

The first book of the *Science of Logic* is *The Doctrine of Being*. The latter begins (first section) with *determinateness* [*déterminité*], itself determined as *quality*. The first moment of quality (first chapter) is *being* as such, in its indeterminate immediacy.—The necessity of beginning, which the introductory text of the first book has prescribed, is thus actualized (*With What Must the Science Begin?*): the point of departure of philosophy can only be simple immediacy, in which any expression [*Ausdruck*] of the absolute cannot be anything other than "an empty word and only being"

(*SL*, 78). Being in its immediacy is the emptiness of all the words
that could determine it. The movement of the first chapter from
the introductory text, which is not yet part of the process itself, up
to the text of the Remark, will thus be—as much as the dialectics
of being and nothing—the passage from the emptiness of words to
the excessive wealth of *one* word, of the word that, as the Remark
says, goes further than any other words of the same kind. But at the
same time, just as it is in two "detached" texts that an emphasis is
placed on words, the dialectics of being will never be presented as
a dialectic of language. This does not mean, however, that language, words, or, at least, remarks on words will not intervene in
the first chapter—on the contrary, as we shall see. What one must
therefore attempt to read in that chapter, in order to get to the
Remark, is the functioning, in the primordial dialectical process,
of a (not rigorously, not expressly) dialectical process that pertains
to—or that is based on—language, or words.

The dialectics of being, as such, occurs in three rather brief
stages, which are the three paragraphs of the chapter. The first two
posit the identity of being and nothing in the indifferent and
empty simplicity of their immediacy. The third paragraph establishes the truth of this identity as the passing over of the one into
the other, that is to say, the vanishing [*Verschwinden*] of the one in
the other: *becoming*. Becoming itself unfolds in three moments: 1.
Unity of Being and Nothing; 2. *Moments of Becoming: Coming-to-be
and Ceasing-to-be*; 3. *Sublation of Becoming*. Four long Remarks (altogether longer than the whole chapter with its three paragraphs)
are annexed to the first moment, and the *Remark on aufheben*
(longer than the second and third paragraphs that precede it) is appended to the third moment. Before the Remark on the word, the
concept has thus entered well into discourse, and it has done so
through its two appellations *aufheben* and *Moment* (the latter being
the fitting, acceptable one—*passend*—when the concept finds itself

in the "more particular determination" of "something reflected").[5]
It has entered into discourse as (or "in") the second and third moment (subparagraphs) of the third stage of the first sequence of the
dialectic of the *Science of Logic* (paragraph: *becoming*). In other
words, it has entered into discourse as (or "in") the determination
of what only begins to be the truth, according to what Hegel writes
at the start of *Becoming*: "What is the truth is neither being nor
nothing, but that being—does not pass over but has passed over
[*übergangen ist*]—into nothing, and nothing into being" (*SL*, 82–
83). The *aufheben* will be the concept of the movement of truth or,
more precisely, of the passage as truth. Now, the truth of this passage, Hegel says here and repeats elsewhere, is that it has always
already come to pass [*c'est qu'il (s')est toujours déjà passé*].[6] It has
therefore actually preceded the exposition of its truth and the denomination—*aufheben*—through which this exposition takes
place. But if the exposition, as *plastic* exposition, is the genuine
place of truth—speculative presentation—one must therefore understand both the truth of the *aufheben* through the already-past
of becoming [*le déjà-passé du devenir*] and the becoming already-
past through (or "as") truth that exposes itself by *aufheben* [by
sublating].

Aufheben is the truth of a past, the being-past [*l'être-passé*] of truth,
yet Hegel does not expressly determine his concept through this
trait. On the other hand, it is indeed under the heading, or the law,
of this always-past [*toujours-passé*] that the *aufheben* posits its word
and is inscribed in the text. One cannot but have noticed the singular syntax of the first sentence of the Remark: "*To sublate*
[*aufheben*] and the *sublated* [*das Aufgehobene*] . . . constitute one of
the most important concepts": a plural works as a singular[7]—one
concept is made up of (or in any case is designated by) the infinitive
of a verb (not even nominalized) *and* the past participle in the pas-

sive form of that verb. The Hegelian *Aufheben* is almost always, in Hegel's text, a verb (rather than the noun *Aufhebung*)—and simultaneously, a verb in the past and in the present tense. Or rather, since the two verb tenses [*modes verbaux*] are forcibly distinguished—whether it is a matter of the operation ("What is sublated is not thereby reduced to nothing"), or of its result ("what is sublated is at the same time preserved")—one could say that the *aufheben* is referred to as the permanent passage of its verb to the past tense and to the passive mode. For such an operation lies wholly in its result, and since, moreover, this result consists entirely in the preservation of the operation, as far as the latter is twofold, and that what it brings about is the simultaneity of these two aspects (a simultaneity that, under a single concept, is a consubstantiality). On the one hand, the operation, the sublation, the truth of the already-past [*déjà-passé*] is given only when its double component (or "nature") is given, that is, actualized—on the other hand, the result, the sublated, hands over only its double operation. If, then, we confine ourselves to the word or, more precisely, to the double word, the double form *aufheben/aufgehoben*, the *Aufhebung* is both something that has already happened and something that still has to happen. This first "modality" could well be a first determination or a first effect of what the Remark first observes, namely, that this "important concept . . . repeatedly occurs everywhere [throughout the whole of philosophy]." The "return" [*Wiederkehr*] of the *aufheben* is always the return of a past, or the return to the past, unless it be the return of a still-to-come [*un encore-à-venir*]: in any case the return of a passage insofar as it has happened or will have happened [*en tant qu'il (s')est passé, ou qu'il (se) sera passé*]. In some way the *aufheben* has thus already raised the question of its presence.

But we have after all so far only been preoccupied with the word. We still have to examine how the concept is produced and is determined from it—in the space that stretches between the first truth of becoming to the Remark on the *aufheben*.

Whatever the case, this first truth has not formally been presented as an *aufheben* but rather as an *auflösen*—or *aufgelöstsein*— a "resolving" [*dissoudre*] or "having been resolved": this "truth is, therefore, . . . a movement in which both are distinguished [*unterschieden*], but by a difference which has equally immediately resolved itself [*aufgelöst hat*]" (*SL*, 83). As the third moment will show (*Sublation of Becoming*), the relation between difference and its resolution, unfolded for itself (while it is still here only presented in itself [*en soi*]) and articulated into its moments, will constitute becoming—that is to say, according to a first determination of the latter, the *aufheben* itself. *Resolution* thus occupies, in the initial moment of immediacy, the place of *sublation*, the place to which sublation should return [*faire retour*], even if nothing here or elsewhere joins sublation to resolution, that is, sublates this resolution. The difficulty could also be stated in the following manner: the beginning requires an immediate form of *aufheben* anterior and exterior to the *aufheben* itself. Henceforth, the already-happened of the *Aufgehobensein* comes down to be *aufgelöst*—resolved—and it is as if the univocity of the resolution, the "return" of the *aufheben*, occurred against the equivocality of its word and of its concept.[8] Yet this difficulty could be only one form of the very general and logical difficulty of the beginning and of completeness, which any discourse after all has to accommodate . . . if Hegelian discourse had not devoted the preceding pages to this difficulty (*With What Must the Science Begin . . .*) in order to resolve it (is it to resolve or to sublate it?)[9] in the joint position of the immediacy of being and of the empty word. According to this first *solution*, the beginning thus takes place before the passage: but, then, what of the being-past of the passage [*l'être-passé du passage*] in relation to the being-past [*être-passé*] of the beginning? As one sees, either the beginning, the *aufheben*, or the one and the other do not recover from it [*ne s'en relèvent pas*].

This is indeed why, in the third Remark, the text (that is to say, being in its exposition) is apparently forced to come back—to return—to the beginning. It does so in order to push aside the first beginning (Parmenides' immediate being, which therefore must not be confused with Hegel's, for this might imply that the immediacy of the latter be no longer simply immediate and its word no longer simply empty . . .), as well as the second (Fichtean) one, which might be the *aufheben* of the former (*SL*, 95). *Aufheben* in which sense? "To cause to cease" and "to lift up [*relever*]" are here possible—and the concept is in any case not specified. But the *aufheben* of the beginning is excluded from both acceptations. What is indeed excluded, in general, by means of the long and sinuous discussion that this Remark carries on with all the philosophemes of the beginning (those of Parmenides, Fichte, Spinoza, Jacobi, Kant, and Plato) is in fact the *question* of the beginning, more precisely the question *how* [*Wie*]? Such a question "demands comprehensibility" [*Begreiflichkeit fragt*] and belongs to "bad habits of reflection" (*SL*, 96). For "the synthesis, which is the point of interest [*Interesse*] . . . , [is an] *immanent* synthesis, synthesis *a priori*—a self-subsistent, self-determined unity of distinct moments. *Becoming* is this immanent synthesis of being and nothing" (*SL*, 96). (Yet, Hegel adds, one must not give to it the *name* of synthesis, which points to an association, therefore, to an exteriority.) And that immanence, the immanent passage that wins our attention, and that, in this text, captures all the philosophemes, up to and including words themselves, provides the conclusion to the Remark in an additional paragraph—a remark of sort to the Remark—which begins in the following manner: "A further remark can be made about the determination of the transition of being and nothing into each other, namely that it is to be understood [*auffassen*] as it is without any further elaboration of the transition by reflection" (*SL*, 103). There is no *question* of the beginning and therefore no question either of the *how* of the beginning of the *aufheben* or of the *aufheben* of the beginning. There is only a *fassen* of it—a grasping [*saisie*] whose complicity with the *aufheben* of reading we already know from the preamble through which we had to go. It is from the very beginning of speculative discourse—it might even be especially at its beginning—that knowledge must return to that discourse in order to "grasp" it. And it is at that initial point, where the science (of logic) has not yet, so to speak, uttered its first word (and especially not the word of its process, the *aufheben*), that this "grasping" is no doubt presented and imposed in the purest manner. One should, without however being able to reconstitute all the reflexive determinations of it, *fassen* the passage where everything begins. One should know—without science— how to read Hegel. That reading is a hearing: one must grasp a voice that is uttered. In the text of the Remark such is indeed the question—it is Jacobi's—to which Hegel will have paid the closest attention in order to challenge or to resolve it, but to resolve it only as a question: "What brings *pure spontaneity* (ego) into oscillation? Whence does its pure vowel get its consonant, or rather how does its *soundless*, uninterrupted *sounding* interrupt itself and break off in order to gain at least a kind of 'self-sound' (vowel), an *accent?*"[10] Hegel's text, which takes on Jacobi's metaphor, if not the question as a question, can therefore be read—or heard (understood)—in the following manner: the unarticulated noise is uttered in its imma- nence, the voice sounds by itself with the voice [*sonne d'elle-même avec la voix*], the voice passes over into the voice, or, as one might say today (as if one were thus saying something else, which might not always be the case), *it speaks* [ça parle].[11] It does indeed speak in passing, and it passes in speaking; it begins and becomes more pronounced in this way [*ça s'accentue*]. Insofar as sublation has already lost itself [*s'est déjà abîmée*] in the beginning, the beginning of the *aufheben* is a voice, a language or a word, that is uttered and becomes more pronounced by itself, without origin and without grammar.

Insofar as sublation has nevertheless still to be produced [*est encore à produire*], we still have to hear—or to read—in the text the word *aufheben* producing itself [*se produisant tout seul*]. Having begun without having been pronounced, it is pronounced without having begun.

In the first Remark of the chapter—devoted to nothing, to existence, and to God—the word is pronounced, by sheer chance, or at least as though purely inadvertently on the part of the author, in a set phrase that does not allow him any slippage of meaning [*écart de sens*]. Hegel writes concerning the Kantian critique of the ontological proof: "When for example a fuss is made about the hundred [thalers]" ("Wenn namlich ein Aufhebens von den hundert Talern gemacht wird . . .")(*SL*, 89). *Aufheben* here has only a positive value, which is marked in a ready-made expression (*ein Aufhebens machen*) and is therefore even more strictly delimited. The first *aufheben* of the text is an accident, a mere writing mechanism. . . . —But the reader might not even have paid attention to it if the following occurrences of the word were to occupy a clearer position.

But that is not exactly the case. Everything would yet lead us to expect the exhibition of the word (and first of all, as we shall see, of one word, whichever it may be), with all the precision and the wealth of its concept. The second Remark does indeed turn to the insufficiency of certain expressions for rendering the unity of being and nothing in becoming. This insufficiency is above all that of the proposition "being and nothing are one and the same," since "the emphasis is laid chiefly on their being one and the same [Eins-und-dasselbe-*sein*]" (*SL*, 90), which constitutes only a unilateral determination. The proposition is therefore marked by a defect—an excess—of emphasis [*défaut d'accent*].[12] It can be accentuated only with difficulty; it is not, as it should be, the accent of the passage—and Hegel indeed seizes the occasion to state: "In this connection we must, at the outset, make this general observation [*Bemerkung*], namely, that the proposition in the *form of a judgement* is not suited [*geschickt*] to express [*ausdrücken*] speculative truths" (*SL*, 90). The fate that, from the outset, condemns the whole order of proposition is without appeal (we are beginning to be familiar with this Hegelian preamble . . .). There is no question of making good for it (*ergänzen*, to complete or to make up for) by positing the reverse proposition: for the two propositions might thus remain without effective link [*unverbunden*].—And it is at this point that, abandoning the *Satz* to its fate, Hegel turns to a word. That word is *unity* [*Einheit*], and it is, "so to speak, [an] unfortunate word [*unglückliches Wort*]" (*SL*, 91). Once again, then, fate strikes language. . . . Indeed, unity points to the exterior reflection and even to exterior action, which compare and unite two objects. "Unity, therefore, expresses wholly *abstract* sameness [*Dieselbigkeit*] and sounds [*lautet*] all the more blatantly paradoxical [*auffalend*, which attracts notice, surprising] the more the terms of which it is asserted show [*sich zeigen*] themselves to be sheer opposites" (ibid.). Now, nothing is more differentiated than being and nothing: unless one fall into abstraction, their unity must therefore be indicated without the designation and the meaning of *unity*. And perhaps even without recourse to any designation.[13] Could there be some other suitable word? It does not seem so. Hegel only adds: "So far then, it would be better to say only *unseparatedness* [*Ungetrenntheit*] and *inseparability* [*Untrennbarkeit*], but then the affirmative aspect of the relation of the whole would not find expression" (*SL*, 91). . . . The inquiry about words is already over. But if, concerning propositions and their combinations, Hegel seems to have laid down a law—the law of the speculative insufficiency of all the grammatical copulas, of the *is* and the *and*—concerning words, however, nothing tells us that we have the principle of an exhaustive analysis of the lexicon. One is rather handed over to the regime of a production of samples—as if in passing—which remains suspended between the a priori position of a law and the beginning of an induction and which can just as well be considered the pushing aside of a bad lexicon before the production of the "good" one.—But all that we can in fact say is that Hegel now gives up—words and propositions.

> (*In some way, one might consequently ask: how, in these conditions, can one continue to read? Or else: in the name of what and by what means can one question Hegel? But one can also ask: what should one rather give up: reading—or questions about it, their interrogative form?*)

An inquiry is thus exhausted without having come to an end. And yet, having given up, Hegel can conclude. Truth is finally told; it is told through an entire paragraph, the first one of the text that "truly" obeys the Hegelian syntax and lexicon, the first one concerning which a literary critic might say, without hesitation, that it really arises out of Hegel's style—and the first one where *aufheben* is pronounced, or is written.

Thus the whole true result which we have here before us is *becoming*, which is not merely the one-sided or abstract unity of being and nothing. It consists rather in this movement, that pure being is immediate and simple, and for that very reason is equally pure nothing, that there *is* a difference between them, but a difference which no less sublates [*aufhebt*] itself and *is not*. The result, therefore, equally asserts the difference of being and nothing, but as a merely fancied or imagined difference [*nur gemeintein*]. (*SL,* 92)

Aufheben here above all means "to cause to cease." The difference—which is not the active, productive *Differenz* but rather the distinction, the separation, *Unterschied*—is suppressed as actual or conceptual difference. It thus appears in the result as mere opinion. Beyond, that is, with the help of the *aufheben* truth rules.

One can henceforth go more quickly through the text of the first chapter. The *aufheben* will not be determined otherwise up until the end of the third moment: its verb will constantly designate the suppression of difference, that is to say, also, of the unilateral determination in general. It simply turns out that the text will no longer mention the status of *opinion* that the determination takes once it is suppressed. Hegel will give this up too—in this way avoiding characterizing further the movement of the *aufheben* as an elevation from an inferior to a superior degree but at the same time also avoiding characterizing this movement in any other definite manner. It looks as though, with the *aufheben* of unilaterality and of its difference in being-and-nothing, the *aufheben* of the unilaterality of the *aufheben*, whatever it may be, might have also occurred and, consequently, the *aufheben* of the possibility of differentiating *aufheben*. *Aufheben* is not, or is hardly, distinguishable: in order to see it while reading the text one must want or know how to see it.

Hegelian discourse will have said nothing about it. It is yet the only one that succeeds *in saying* something: for if the *aufheben* is the suppression of the difference of being and nothing, it is the suppression of the difference concerning which Hegel challenges his critics *to say* what it is (*SL*, 92). The *aufheben* stands out [*s'enlève*] against the background of an impossible saying [*parole*], of an unsayable difference, unsayable because one cannot *define* being and nothing. One can at the most *picture* [*vorstellen*] the one as "pure light" and the other as "pure night" (*SL*, 93), but one will nevertheless be immediately forced to recognize that "in absolute clearness there is seen as much, and as little, as in absolute darkness" (ibid.) and that, consequently, "something can be distinguished only in determinate light or darkness (light is determined by darkness and so is darkened light, and darkness is determined by light, is illuminated darkness), and for this reason, that it is only darkened light and illuminated darkness which have within themselves the moment of difference and are, therefore, *determinate* being" (ibid.). The *aufheben*, which is hardly distinguishable, does not follow on from difference—which is always already resolved in it [*résorbée*]—but precedes and makes possible difference. *Aufheben* is the possible saying that rises within the chiaroscuro—it is the very voice of philosophy, the doleful cry of the owl at twilight.

And this howl is determined, if one dare say so, merely by being itself—or, in any case, by being the fact or the process of a "self." In some way the only distinctive mark of the *aufheben* might indeed be the reflexive form in which the verb is most often pronounced. The *aufheben* is a *sich aufheben* of difference, as we read a moment ago, and if the content of the verb remains little determined, the text however puts all the accent on the *sich*, on the autonomy of the *aufheben*. We should even say, no doubt, that the counterpart to the indeterminacy of the *aufheben*—if determination indeed implies the exteriority of a determining instance—is nothing other than its aseity [*aséité*]. The voice of the *aufheben* takes on its accent in a *sich*, and whatever the subject of the *aufheben* be (whether it be what it in fact always is . . . the unsayable subject that difference constitutes), it is only ever *aufgehoben* insofar as it *sich aufhebt*. It sublates itself.—The first movement of becoming ends in this way: "but we call dialectic the higher movement of reason in which such seemingly [*solche Scheinende*] utterly separate terms pass over into each other spontaneously, through that which they are, a movement in which the presupposition sublates itself. It is the dialectical immanent nature of being and nothing themselves to manifest their unity, that is, becoming their truth" (ibid., 105). The *aufheben* is essentially *what goes without saying* [*ce qui va de soi*] and, at the same time, what passes or causes to pass by itself [*ce qui, de soi, va, ce qui passe ou fait passer*]—the reciprocal and spontaneous vanishing [*Verschwinden*] of that which does not constitute any stable state, not even an intermediary one (and we were able, in passing, to challenge with Hegel yet another term: "state [*Zustand*] is here an unsuitable [*unpassend*], barbarous expression" [ibid., 104]).—Vanished, or more precisely vanishing, being and nothing are henceforth presented (it is the second moment of becoming) as sublated [*des* relevés] [*aufgehobene*], that is, as *moments*: "They sink [*herabsinken*] from their initially imagined *self-subsistence* [*Selbstständigkeit*] to the status of *moments*, which are still *distinct*, but at the same time are sublated" (ibid., 105). *Moment* is therefore the name of what is different [*le différent*], the difference of which is already suppressed, or rather has already been suppressed. *Aufheben* is the name of the suppression of the states that are sublated into moments, and the *aufheben* into *moments* tells of the difference whose mere positing—whose concept, one could add—remained, as such, forever unsayable. It is thus possible to understand that the suppressed difference is at the same time preserved. But in order to read it, or to hear it being said, here too one had to want to or to know how to hear it—one had to have so fine a hearing as no longer exactly to be able to hear the differentiated meaning of certain words and that the *aufheben* pass without being exposed to (as a) determination. All this goes without saying, and it does so increasingly hastily in the text, where, from now on, *sublation* ceaselessly functions, accelerates, and tightens its functioning right at the level of the *self* and, in a certain way, as if it formed ipseity, or better, the process of the ipseity of the *self* itself, since "each sublates itself in itself and is in its own self the opposite of itself" (ibid., 106).

Becoming, then, goes without saying [*va donc de soi*] through an *aufheben* and as an *aufheben*. In this identification nothing has taken place that might allow us rigorously to recognize a conceptual construction. On the contrary: a word, then another, has come to operate where all determinations were missing—in the concept and in the proposition of unity—where every determination *had* to be missing by virtue of the law of the beginning. The *aufheben*, consequently, had to pass by or to take place beside [*passe ou se passe à côté*] the play of determinations. And it is indeed what has happened: its word has slipped into the text, without a word [*sans rien dire*], and when it has come to exhibit itself, it was already too late for its concept—or better, it was too late for a concept to be determined (through a definition of word or an articulation of propositions). *Aufheben* has taken over [*pris la relève*] from an impossible function: determination. It has always been too early or too late for determining the takeover itself: and it is clear that this double impossibility itself goes without saying. This is why it equally goes without saying that the whole logic of *sublation* has occurred in the sliding of a word and in the slipping of the text on this word, which should moreover be understood in every sense: the text has slid along, has advanced [*s'est avancé*]—but in a lateral or evasive movement—thanks to this word, and the text has slid over this word with an astonishing discretion, as over what one must know how to understand without anything having to be spelled out. . . . The whole necessity of the *aufheben* has, up until now, been held in this discretion; it has kept itself in these slidings, these imperceptible displacements, in the play of vanishing apparitions, which will have, in fact, constituted the entire text in the manner of an infinitesimal calculus, whose example Hegel has precisely invoked.[14] For infinitesimal magnitudes constitute this "pure concept," whose determination or whose being merges with the "vanishing." As a concept, sublation will at least have—once more, *in passing*—been illustrated through infinitesimal magnitude; but from the strictly conceptual point of view, the illustration is itself only a "vanishing magnitude."[15] The discourse of the *aufheben* is justified only by comparison with another discourse, and very precisely, with the discourse of a calculus; discreetly, the *aufheben* appears to liken itself or to become analogous to this series of magnitudes, whose infinite decreasing diminishes the (mathematical) discretion without, however, canceling it out. But in spite of everything, nothing in the text allows one to say that the *aufheben* might be properly *calculated*, which would come down, in this case, to being *derived*; the calculation of sublation, if there be, is nothing but the sliding, or the "slid" [*glissé*] of its word, and consequently, nothing allows us to cancel out a difference, perhaps itself infinitely small . . . , that persists in separating this textual calculation [*calcul*] from the other.[16]

Such a difference takes nothing away, however, from the proximity of the two calculi or from the precision of textual calculation. For the latter does not come to an end. If it is indeed too late for determining the *aufheben*, that is, for determining becoming inasmuch as it "is" an *aufheben*, this must just as well mean that the *aufheben* cannot be determined by becoming, cannot be resolved [*résoudre*] in the image of a flux[17] or in the notion of a progression, but that it is rather the *aufheben* that must have taken hold of becoming and have resolved it [*l'avoir résolu*]. And it is precisely what happens in the third moment, *Sublation of Becoming*, where the vanishing of difference occurs, by itself [*de lui-même*], as "the vanishing of becoming or the vanishing of the vanishing itself" (*SL*, 106), a movement that, of course, does not constitute a return to the empty determination of nothing (or to the determination of the emptiness of nothing) but that, on the contrary, engenders the passage to the *determinate being* [*Dasein*]—or, more precisely, that produces the being-already-past in determinate being [*l'être-déjà-passé dans l'être-là*]. Here again, the impeccable precision of the textual calculus does not fail: on the one hand, the *aufheben*, as the suppression of difference, is indeed well suppressed, and one returns to difference (which one had, if only abstractly, never left . . .), which is now posited as the unilaterality of the *moments*. But the *moment* is nothing other than the *aufgehoben*, the suppressed *as such*, if one dare say so (Hegel precisely and quite rightly does not dare to do so: the sublated has no other "identity" than that which the passage through sublation confers upon it). On the other hand, then, the *aufheben* is not suppressed and on the contrary becomes the power that rules the passage, a passage that is from now on, already, a passage over into the following moment—a passage that, in this chapter, has already taken place in the following chapter. This double play of the *aufheben* in turn conforms to an infinitely small difference: the text writes "vanishing of the vanishing," not "*aufheben* of the *aufheben*," that is to say, "suppression of suppression" (if one keeps the most simple and current value that the word after all has always had in this chapter), nor "sublation of sublation" (which might imply a constructed concept of sublation). The text precisely passes between the two. This implies at least two things: first, the *aufheben* does not coincide with itself or close up on itself and thus avoids, additionally, letting itself be identified; second, the *aufheben* is preserved, is carried outside itself; it slips into the rest of the text intact and, so to speak, neither suppressed nor preserved by means of the sole and minimal gap of a word, of another word that slips in, only for a moment, in its place: *verschwinden* instead of *aufheben*. In the vanishing of the *verschwinden* the ultimate possibility of determining the concept of the *Aufhebung* vanishes— and the possibility and the power of the verb *aufheben*, on the other hand, slip in or are presented as preserved.[18]

It is then that one comes upon the *Remark: The Expression "To Sublate."* One sees how the explication de texte will have succeeded in situating it. . . . That whole *detour* was only in order to get to a text in which everything leaves much to be desired (for a concept is missing: but did one have to wait so long for producing it?) and that is put under no obligation (for there is a word, through which everything works).

Through its position the text of the Remark well answers to

these antinomic conditions: a remark is added, is appended to a discourse in the economy of which it intervenes at most only in a minor fashion; but at the same time, the remark at issue takes part in the whole economy of the text and even redoubles it insofar as it constitutes, as we already said, a new passage in the following chapter. That is, insofar as it ends up by presenting the becoming of becoming as its *aufheben* in the first determination or difference of being, that of determinate being. The double functioning of the Remark (which is yet not given as such in Hegel's text, and which must be deciphered in a text that, in certain respects, seems composed of bits and pieces) can be explained, if at all, through one word: *Ausdruck*, expression—the term that designates, at least formally, the object of the Remark. On the one hand, Hegel indeed draws attention to the particularity of an expression that he has just used and whose current usage turns out to be suitable to the philosophical usage, a happy and secondary circumstance that we can celebrate in passing. On the other hand, the Remark sends us back to the positing of *Dasein*, that is to say, to the positing of what has just concluded and carried forward the analysis of the *Sein*; but it does so in order to send us back to the *Ausdruck* of the *Sein* in *Dasein*. The Remark combines—a combination that has apparently no conceptual status—the incidental mention of an expression of becoming and the becoming-its-own-expression of being. As we read: "The more precise meaning and expression which being and nothing receive, now that they are *moments*, is to be ascertained from the consideration of determinate being as the unity in which they are preserved" (ibid., 107–8).

The expression, the *Ausdruck*, is therefore here not simply an appendix. The Remark has added something to the text of the chapter: notably, in the joint regime of the "meaning-and-expression," the *preservation* of being and nothing, which, up until now, had not been formally at issue, even if everything no doubt was implying it. The law that will have ruled the chapter has in this way just been given to us (and with it, the law of the whole progression of the *Science of Logic*): the Remark made us go to what has actually happened [*nous a fait passer à ce qui s'est, en réalité, passé*]. For it is now no longer a question of giving one to understand but rather of giving one to understand accurately, of making one grasp a precise meaning. The Remark has dealt with an *Ausdruck*, so that, as it said, the meaning of the *Ausdruck: aufheben* "be clearly grasped."

Now, at least through the first reading this "grasping of a determinate meaning" has taken place in the simplest manner, which can be reconstituted in the following way: *aufheben*, the term which we just used, is (or expresses)[19] a fundamental concept. We have taken this term in its negative value: to suppress.[20] What matters now is to state more precisely that this negative value is necessarily doubled up by its positive opposite. The *aufheben* preserves. This is indeed what the two acceptations that the word has in German indicate. *Of course*, this concept therefore sends us back to *Dasein*, as to the unity that simultaneously suppresses and preserves being and nothing in their difference.

That—obvious—reading of the Remark consists, consequently, of redoubling the entire text that has preceded it (through which one no doubt now sees better why one had to go) in order to extract from it or to affirm on the basis of it what was not directly, expressly indicated in it as such: the preservation of the terms of the suppressed difference, or of the difference of terms. The Remark appends to the negative process that has led to it a second positive mark—it thus suppresses this process, while preserving it under (or "as") the concept that it determines: *aufheben*. It therefore gives the negative process its status and in this way *sublates* the whole of the first chapter of the *Science of Logic*; that is, it sublates the very possibility of the *Science of Logic* insofar as the latter begins with the empty immediacy of being and of its identity with nothing. At the same time, this second mark, which allows us to "grasp" the "determinate meaning" of the *aufheben*, erases, or delimits, the excess or the lack that continually affects this term (and with it any statement about the truth of beginning) . To sum up, let us say the *aufheben* was therefore both the *suppression* of the immediate beginning, of the autoarticulation of a voice whose "how?" remained unanswered (the *aufheben* has therefore always been uttered [*articulé*]), *and* the *preservation* of the beginning whose suppression, as the suppression of the difference of terms, seemed to challenge the possibility of any discourse to be held. (The *aufheben* thus holds in check [the relation between the parts of] discourse, which otherwise might fall into unilateral abstraction.)

Why does the *aufheben* preserve what it suppresses? To answer this question is to provide the concept of the *aufheben*. The Remark applies itself to doing so: "What is sublated is not thereby reduced to nothing [*Nichts*]. Nothing is *immediate*; what is sublated, on the other hand, is the result of *mediation* [*ein Vermitteltes*] . . . ; it still has, therefore, *in itself* the *determinateness from which it originates*" (ibid., 107). To sublate is therefore to mediate. The concept of the *aufheben* is constructed on the basis of the concept of mediation. What is mediation—*Vermittlung?* One can very well here reread the whole chapter: it has not determined that concept. Or rather, if the *Vermittlung* is a passage through the middle, or the middle-term— *Mitte*—if it is, whatever it may be, a median or an intermediate operation [*médiane ou mitoyenne*], the text will have only told us, in passing (and concerning its proximity to infinitesimal calculus), that there is no intermediate state, no *Mittelzustand*, and that, as we saw, *state* is here "a barbarous expression." There is no *Mitte* or *Mittel* as state—there *is* no middle, the middle *is* not, or else, as Hegel concedes: "to use the same language as that just quoted . . . *there is nothing which is not an intermediate state between being and nothing*" (ibid., 105).—But "the language" is not the right one; its *Ausdruck* is not philosophical; it freezes the pure passage into a "state," the incessant movement of difference that sublates itself.

The *Vermittlung*, if it should like to avoid barbarity (a confused and coarse speech, inaudible for the delicate hearing of the speculative thinker . . .), cannot be established on the basis of a determination of the *Mitte*; it cannot be established in any sense of the word: it cannot be grasped outside of sublation, and the word *mediation*, which has slipped into the determination of the concept of "sublation," does after all nothing but mark for the second time sublation itself—even if this superposition of marks does not enlighten the identity of *sublation* "itself."[21]

In order to double the mark (as one ups the ante) of the *aufheben*, the Remark repeats, in and as the determination of the meaning of the word, the curious functioning of the text to which it is appended. A word slips into it, an extra word, on which the construction of the concept in turn slides and skids. Through the gap between two words, discourse comes near a definition—but this gap is itself a vanishing difference, and the text has already folded one word over the other. There is once more a single word, which is in excess or which is still missing; the calculus is infallible.[22]

From its first paragraph the Remark carries us off course or makes its own conceptual reading slide, disturbs or forbids the grasping (*auffassen*) of meaning. One cannot here read—directly— the first or the second mark of a concept. But one is obliged to follow the re-marked and persistent trace of the text's singular slipping economy. Now, this text—as we saw going through it—brought into play more than one determination, used numerous concepts, made more than one detour. All this goes against the direct reading of the Remark. Just as the text of the chapter—the text of the beginning (of the) dialectic—became legible (as far as it has become so . . .) only in its last Remark, it will be possible to read the Remark itself only once it is re-marked in other texts, which, by themselves, will be articulated to the text of the first chapter, on its excess and its lack. One still has to make detours; one still has to take and (lose) patience.

Remark

Before carrying on, one cannot avoid pointing at least to the other path that the same textual calculation could lead us to follow: no longer from the Remark to the texts, but from the texts to the Remark. The Remarks of the *Science of Logic* have this remarkable feature: a great number of them are devoted to *expressions* and to the pertinence or nonpertinence of these expressions in speculative discourse. In other words: in the *Science of Logic* the treatment of expressions takes place almost exclusively in the appended texts that the Remarks constitute (or occasionally, in texts whose status is somewhat comparable, such as the untitled introduction to the section on objectivity (705–10). In the table of contents only one Remark, in addition to the one on the *Aufheben*, has an *Ausdruck* as a title (the *Ausdruck: Was für eines?* which, in common usage means: "What kind of a Thing?" and literally: "What for a Thing?").—Hegel notes and picks out the apparent oddness—*sonderbar erscheinend*—within the analysis of Being-for-self, insofar as the latter is precisely the Being-for-one (160–64). But many other Remarks deal with expressions, sometimes in order to brush them aside (we have already come up against the word *unity*, as well as the critique of propositions, which will be found elsewhere—[for example, 172 and 410–11]—the same goes for a word such as *herausgehen*, "going forth" [153], for *synthesis* [208], for the "empty talk" of identity both in the word and in the proposition [456–57]—and the same goes above all for expression by means of numbers, mathematical symbols and symbols in general, as well as for the Leibnizian idea of a characteristics, the criticism of which recurs with insistence—[212, 295, 325, 616, 685]—and sometimes to determine them and thus *sublate* their sense (such as is the case for the infinite, 150–51), of the *quantum* borrowed from Latin (186), of "generated magnitudes," one of Newton's metaphors (257), of the proposition "the positive and negative are the same" (435), and more generally, remarks on the mark of the concept, *Merkmal* (613), and on language, which, with a view to this mark, Hegel opposes to symbolic artifices (618).

An economy of Remarks seems to double up the economy of logical discourse: an economy of remarks, that is, a subordinated "detached" dispersed economy that does not obey the strict progression of the concept but rather chance encounters between the text and the good or (ill) fortunes of the writer. For Hegel it also seems to obey the necessity of repeating with insistence certain *motifs*, none of which, let us note, is the object or the process of a definite moment in the order of discourse (that is to say: of the grounds) of the *Science of Logic*. It looks as though these motifs— above all, the motif of *speculative language*—can only be exposed in an appendix or in the margin, just as, for that matter, the general motif of speculative exposition (reading and writing) was exposed in the "partly narrative" Preface to the *Phenomenology of Spirit*. But, by this very fact, it looks as though speculative discourse had to draw attention to its own language, whether it be for noticing its presence in natural language or for underlining the gap from such and such a language (as that of mathematics), and thus had to *draw attention to itself*, as language, in its own appendices.

One could indeed, and one should, expand the whole of this Remark to the analogous texts of the *Encyclopedia*, Remarks and Additions taken from the lectures,[23] where, among others, the text on the word *aufheben* that we have already quoted is found, and the Remarks where the Hegelian theory of the sign and of language is developed a little (we will have to come back to one or to the other of these texts). One could even go from the *Anmerkung* to the *merken*—to mark and to re-mark—in Hegel's text in general and, for example, to this passage of the *Lectures on the Proofs of the Existence of God*, where Hegel criticizes the *Ausdruck: Merkmal*— distinctive mark, feature, characteristic—insofar as it indicates the "subjective purpose" that one pursues by retaining only the determinations of the object that are of use in "marking distinctions [*Merken*]."[24] The *merken* in general is enclosed in its subjectivity and in its word, is unilateral and circular, and misses the object as well as the demonstration. Consequently, we will be able neither to begin to carry through nor to bring to completion the discourse of science (of logic) on the register of the *merken*. Yet Hegel's text does not pass on it [*ne s'en passe pas*] and draws attention to itself through its *Anmerkungen*: herein lies its remarkable character, its unusualness, indeed its oddness: *Merkwürdigkeit*.

3

Speculative Words

All the same, it's no wonder that the majority of people aren't convinced by our arguments [*genoménon to nūn legoménon*], for they've never seen a *man* that fits our *plan* (and the rhymes of this sort they have heard are usually intended [*homoiōména*] and not, like this one, the product of mere chance [*apo tou automatou*). That is to say, they've never seen a man or a number of men who themselves rhymed with virtue [*parisōménon kai ōmoiōménon*].

—Plato, *Republic*

If we take the discourse of the chapter and of its final Remark to their word, we are left with words. What the "important concept" has not, as such, handed over (but to which it has substituted an additional word: *Vermittlung*), "language" gives to us, right in [*à même*] its most current usage: *aufheben* has the double meaning of preserving and of causing to cease—(and if the *Vermittlung* has just "explained" the positivity of the *aufheben*, preservation, it also "explains" its negativity, since "in order to preserve" something, it "is removed from its immediacy," and *vermitteln* is indeed to introduce into the medial or the mediate, to make something become medial or mediate, to negate immediacy. One cannot fail to notice, however, that if, on the one hand, one were really to put this explanation to work, it would bring us back to the difficulty of the medial "state," or of mediation *as such*, and that, on the other

hand, the text of the Remark works in the order of the comparison and no longer in the order of the concept alone: "something
is removed from its immediacy and so from an existence [*Dasein*]
which is open to external influences, in order to preserve it" (*SL*,
107). Now, this describes wonderfully the thoroughly empirical art
of making preserves, which, in all rigor, cannot however quite be
a suitable practice for the concept, if only because the latter must
accomplish a *sich aufheben* . . .).

Henceforth, the word will bear everything—and, first and foremost, it will bear the *Aufhebung* "itself." And as if in order to avoid
that we be mistaken about it (or in order to disconcert any search
for the concept . . .), Hegel insists on it, by amending the Remark
in the second edition, where he adds no less than four sentences on
this word. These sentences say the following: first, it is possible to
present "the two *definitions* [déterminations]" of *aufheben* as "two
dictionary *meanings*" (Hegel's emphasis); that way of presenting
things is an *aufführen*, a representation, a staging. The stage of the
lexicon is, for example, the dictionary, which gives two distinct and
successive meanings [*significations*] of the word, numbering them
when necessary. But this staging is only a possibility ("can be"), and
the lexicon here represents a limited point of view, too limited no
doubt for what speculative thought finds in (the meaning of)
aufheben. It is at least what the text almost certainly says, for the
latter becomes rather curiously difficult to understand. The text
goes on: "But it is certainly remarkable [*auffallend*, striking, spec-
tacular] to find that a language has come to use one and the same
word for two opposite meanings." This statement can be understood in two ways (which are themselves opposed . . .): either, on
the stage of the dictionary, it would be appropriate to note the
spectacular character of that word, to draw attention to the way in
which language somewhat overindulges with it [*l'excès, en quelque
sorte, auquel se porte avec lui la langue*]; this is what one usually forgets and to what speculative thought will be devoted. Or else, the

lexical stage is at once improbable and insufficient: in exercising its
function of attaching a word to a meaning [*signification*], a language cannot give itself over to such deviations [*écarts*]—up to the
point of subverting the signifying function itself—and it is in any
case outside the lexical stage that speculative thought will put language into play. These two ways of reading or of accentuating the
sentence are manifestly undecidable. But the text itself does help
us to decide. Incidentally, the two emphases are not incompatible:
whether it be a question of a spectacular "set up" played on the lexical stage [*un coup monté et joué sur la scène du lexique*], of a crossing of this stage, or still of an unprecedented shrinking back of its
limits, an exceptional and exorbitant functioning of meaning
[*signification*] is still at issue. All this remains possible—and unde-
cided—in the following sentence: "It is a delight to speculative
thought to find in the language words which have in themselves a
speculative meaning; the German language has a number of such"
(*SL*, 107). Nothing is thus clarified concerning the surprise of the
spectacular offered in the lexicon or in relation to it. It is rather the
surprise itself that is somewhat converted and transformed into a
happy surprise "for speculative thought": this thought "finds" *its*
meaning," its "speculative meaning" "right at the level" of the
word.[1] Chance and happiness reign where one expected the analysis of an accident or of an excess of language. The happiness is even
double, for to the general case of an apparently always possible find
one must add the chance of German's particular wealth of speculative words. The last sentence added by Hegel insists on this:
"The double meaning of the Latin *tollere* (which has become famous through the Ciceronian pun [*Witz, trait d'esprit*]: *tollendum
esse Octavium*) does not go so far; its affirmative determination
signifies only a lifting-up."[2] If, then, one can find elsewhere a double meaning closely related to that of the *aufheben*, the latter retains
the privilege of the greatest wealth: *tollere* covers an antinomic duality (to suppress, to push aside *or* to lift up); *aufheben* combines a

dialectical or speculative duplicity (to suppress *and* to preserve). (Ultimately, one should understand the difference of degree the text establishes between the two words, as a genuine difference of kind . . .). Consequently, *tollere* remains caught in the spectacular character of a word that sends us back to "two opposite meanings [*Bestimmungen*]," and the help of a *Witz*, of play, is needed for staging this duality. Besides the fact that the *play on words* might lack seriousness (we shall come back to that), it is what gives rise to confusion precisely because it functions through the antinomy of meaning [*significations*]. In the Addition to § 96 of the *Encyclopedia*, which we quoted, Hegel said: "This ambiguity in linguistic usage, through which the same word has a negative and a positive meaning, cannot be regarded as an accident nor yet as a reason to reproach language as if it were a source of confusion [*Verwirrung*]. We ought rather to recognise here the speculative spirit of our language . . ." (*Enc. I*, § 96:154). On the one hand, the chance that presides over the finding of such words in our language does not involve chance as the "law" of formation of these words but rather the "speculative spirit" of language itself; on the other hand, the *aufheben* is not confused, muddled—one does not make use of confusion. Where the *Witz* introduces an equivocation, the word *aufheben* and its like have or are by themselves the clarity and the distinction of the "speculative spirit" that inhabits, in person, German language.[3]

And it is indeed the very clarity of the speculative that the Hegelian "demonstration," which we just witnessed, possesses. Everything is resolved in it thanks to and in the speculative. It is the speculative that gives rise to or that creates a space distinct from the lexical stage, that recognizes the speculative meaning of such and such a word, that inhabits "our language," and it is for it that there is chance, happiness, and satisfaction. The *speculative* was thus already concealed behind the pressing invitation to *grasp* the meaning of *aufheben* with which the Remark opened. From the outset the latter is thus addressed to the speculative reader and to no one else. (The Remark may be further characterized: what if, far from being "exoteric," it were "esoteric," reserved to those who "grasp," whispered to the finest ears, and forbidden to those who are not, as Hegel wrote a few pages earlier, in the trust or in the confidence of speculative thought.)[4] For that reader the speculative can now slip in, as an extra word, which will have carried the decision of the text, by subtracting it—without meeting any opposition—from uncertainties, from the astonishments, indeed from the confusions into which it was entering. For the decision ultimately rests on the epithet *speculative*, which is attached to *meaning* [*signification, Bedeutung*]. In winning this epithet, meaning would seem to have been torn away from the ordinary status of language, that of the correspondence of a word to *one* determination, and torn away from the surprising staging of *two* meanings. What is at issue is in fact *another* meaning—another mode of meaning, or something other than meaning; it is too early to tell. In any case "a speculative meaning" is the singular, the singular singularity of the speculative.

This speculative singularity is singular, above all, in that it immediately, and paradoxically, commits us to a multiplicity. Through the passage to the speculative the threads of the discourse on the *aufheben* suddenly come to weave a complex network, whose internal plurality does not let itself immediately be resolved. The lexical point of view is juxtaposed (or is combined?) to that of speculative thought, since the "decision" of which we spoke did not formally lift the indecision of the text, and "two meanings" in the "use" of a word are juxtaposed (or are combined?) to a "meaning" present "right at the level" of the word [*à même le mot*]. Language in general seems to be able to offer such finds, but German language is particularly rich in this respect; one is thus within the plurality of languages, and *aufheben* is no longer alone within the German one. The text of the Remark will go deeper into this multiplicity, since it will attach to the *aufheben*, and for the "more particular determination [*Bestimmung*]"⁵ of the *aufgehobensein*, the "fitting" appellation (*passend*, passable, acceptable) of *Moment*. That is, it will attach the use of a term that, in German, is after all nothing but the literal transcription of a Latin word—and of a term that, as he notes, Hegel proposes in the second edition by borrowing it from the properties of the lever. We shall come back later to the end of the text. For the moment one has to hand oneself over to the multiplicity that has abruptly been scattered throughout the text.

The question "What is speculative meaning?" is multiplied. For us, readers of Hegel, this means that it is repeated. Let us indeed recall that when, by way of a preamble, we were interrogating Hegel on the modalities of his reading, he was answering by saying that only an *aufheben* of the ordinary grammar of propositions, on condition that it be "expressed," might give us the "speculative *in act*" in its "speculative presentation." Could the word *aufheben* itself alone be that presentation? Hegel might have been prepared to say so, and in any case, in the passage of the *Phenomenology* that we have already quoted, he writes: "The *Aufheben* exhibits [*Darstellt*] its true twofold meaning. . . ."⁶ The exhibition corresponds—if it is not identified with it—to the presence, in the Remark, of "speculative meaning" "*right at the level*" of certain words [*an ihnen selbst*]. We just saw, however, that this presence is presented only to "speculative thought" and only by means of a settlement or an obscure unsettlement of scores with the usual regime of meaning, whether it be "double" or not. We just reread, moreover, that speculative presence does not, in language or languages, absolutely fall to *aufheben*, and we finally noted that, for its determination, *aufheben* comes to attach another word to itself—*Moment*—whose regime of meaning is yet slightly different. Speculative meaning does not therefore amount to the presentation by a word of two meanings—and, reciprocally, speculative

Darstellung does not apparently consist of any determinate mode of meaning, whether it be simple or double, literal or figurative. The meaning of the speculative *Darstellung* is not—at least not exactly—the presentation of *meaning* [*sens*] . . . except in the speculative sense of this term, which remains to be established.— Consequently, things are not as simple as the sentence from the *Phenomenology* might have led us to believe. Rather, it is important to note that Hegel did precisely not content himself with this sentence—let us say with the simple characterization of the *aufheben* as speculative presentation—but that he has, on numerous occasions, displaced, complicated, and multiplied the proposition (and in every sense of this term).

It is no doubt here that the effort to grasp—*auffassen*—the Hegelian *aufheben* encounters a major obstacle or suddenly no longer has any hold. *Aufheben* is indeed *the* word of Hegelian discourse, the *right* word of speculative thought, its password.[7] But that word does not present its meaning—speculative meaning, or speculativity as meaning—in the pure transparency of its presence as word, of its lexical and semantic position. If the Hegelian text comes very close to this solution—which indeed might be the solution to all our difficulties and to that of the Hegelian text—it nevertheless does not opt for it. That is, it does not opt for the metaphysical or magical solution (in this case at least, it would seem to be the same) of the perfect, absolute word, of the resorption in a word of the gap from the sign to the thing. To the very extent that the regime of the *aufheben*, as a speculative word, is presented as distinct from the regime and the stage of meaning [*signification*], it does not correspond either to this traditional *acme* of meaning, whereby the exteriority and the referential function of the sign vanish in the presence and in the transparency, within itself, of the thing. To use the founding categories of the tradition of Plato's *Cratylus*, one is obliged to say that if the *aufheben* is not, from the speculative thinker's point of view, a conventional word [*thesei*]—unless one should adopt surprising conventions on the lexical stage—neither is it a natural word [*phusei*]. With respect to the two poles of philosophical semiology, *aufheben* adopts, if you like, the tactic of the "neither . . . nor." (And this is why Hegel can successively rely on one or the other of these poles and, by a singularly complex movement through which the text gets itself tangled up, move away from meaning while referring to the meanings of the word.)[8]

If the *aufheben*, then, presents itself above all in its verb form— and it is not a coincidence if it does so—it is however not the Word of God. *Aufheben* is not for all that the Son of God, even though it is not a child of chance either. Hence, concerning the *aufheben*, Hegel does not state what he however states concerning God in 1831, the very year he revises the Remark of the *Science of Logic*: "In the Christian religion, it is known that God has revealed Himself, and it is the very nature of God to reveal Himself."[9] Hegel here does not say, "The meaning of *sublating* [relever] (the sublated [*relevé*] of the *aufheben* in speculation) is precisely that everything is sublatable." The *Aufheben* is not the *Offenbarung*—and the reader in quest of revelation must here renounce either the text that he is reading or his own quest. Hegel's text does not give us anything by grace.—This is also why it is not possible to report, to tell Hegel's bon mot either as a good story or as the Good News.

We must therefore go through all its defiles. The question of speculative meaning is multiplied; as a question, it is multiple, and it creates less the determinate process of an answer than the proliferation of its own forms and of its reasons [*attendus*].

That is to say, to begin (or to begin again), that it gives rise to a multiplication of texts. The passage added by Hegel in 1831 to the Remark indeed does not come on its own—as we have already said. Hegel also wrote a second preface, whose first pages turn out to have already (for the reader of this edition) put forward some of the motifs that the Remark consequently repeats.[10] From the opening of that preface Hegel underlines that "the forms of thought are, in the first instance, . . . stored [*niedergelegt*] in human *language* [*Sprache*]" (*SL*, 31). Language [*le langage ou la langue*] is thus logic itself "clearly determined as such [*herausgearbeitet*]" (ibid.). And yet (or henceforth?—the hesitation will be preserved but not sublated . . .); "it is an advantage when a language possesses an abundance of logical expressions, that is, specific and separate expressions for the thought determinations themselves" (*SL*, 32).

The logical wealth is therefore not uniformly distributed, or rather, it is not deposited and "stored" equally in every language.[11] A language may have an advantage—a *Vorteil*, a supplementary share, a greater resource or benefit—over others. Hegel simultaneously holds a twofold discourse (which is also preserved but not sublated . . .) concerning the nature or the provenance of this advantage. On the one hand, a language is precisely indebted to its linguistic system for its logical wealth or poverty (and the preface speaks of particules, signs of inflection, substantives and verbs—and in passing feels sorry for the Chinese language . . .); on the other hand—and as we read elsewhere—what gives a language its logical wealth is a "speculative spirit." But one does not decide on the anteriority—the interiority—of such a spirit over the linguistic system. From the outset, then, everything begins or is determined by an emphasis on language [*une mise en relief de la langue*], which suspends and defers a certain number of traditional questions on language, especially at the threshold of a philosophical work (for example, the questions of expression, of definitions, of the genre of discourse, etc.). But it is German language that deserves the greatest attention:

In this respect German has many advantages [*viele Vorzüge*] over other modern languages; some of its words even possess the further peculiarity of having not only different but opposite meanings so that one cannot fail to recognize a speculative spirit of the language in them: it can delight a thinker to come across [*stossen auf*] such words and to find the union of opposites naïvely shown in the dictionary as one word with opposite meanings, although this result of speculative thinking is nonsensical [*widersinnig*] to the understanding. (*SL*, 32)

As we see, the text of the Remark is repeated. We could say that it is repeated word for word—or rather, that each of its words is underlined, if one of them were not however missing: *aufheben*, the word of the Remark. The general privilege of German precedes and pluralizes—in advance, in the preface—the propriety of the word *aufheben*. Or better, the speculativity, whose concept and word is the *aufheben*, first appears as German's "speculative spirit." The *aufheben* is not mentioned (the preface no doubt also "partly narrative" too forestalls its concept) because here, as an isolated word, it is numbered among all the German words that possess the "further peculiarity" of the "union of opposites," that is, of the *aufheben*. *Aufheben* designates sublation, but the German language has many sublating words, including *aufheben*, as we shall see later. Or rather, the German language behaves as though it had already, if one dare say so, "speculated"—but "speculated" naïvely, according to a "naïvety" homologous to the concept of *aufheben* (without the question of the notion of a "naïve speculation" ever being clarified or sublated . . .).—For all these reasons the "speculative spirit" shows itself, strictly speaking, neither as the "ground," as the "origin," nor as the "structure" of language—nor does it utter *a* word that might be *its* name. If the "result of speculation" is the "property" of German, what is at issue is a singular property that is dispersed discreetly through the lexicon and upon which one might fortunately fall.

Hence, Hegel's reader is unlikely to be able to get around this property. But he cannot avoid venturing into it. As we know, he will then fall upon many words whose list, for once, is worth making—not a catalogue, of course, but rather a somewhat long list, since one must here reckon with the speculative plural. Let us enumerate, then, at first, words with opposite meanings [*significations*] that are the closest to the *aufheben* (not without noting, however, that none of them achieves the "precision" of *aufheben*, in which case, one might have to suspect that, in the preface, Hegel dissimulates a single word under the heading of a plurality . . .): *Abgrund*, the ultimate ground and the bottomless abyss (*SL*, 483—cf. also 475); *Sinn*, "wonderful [*wunderbar*]" word, which means "the organ of immediate apprehension," as well as "the significance, the thought, the universal underlying the thing" (*A*, 1:128–29); and perhaps also *Geschichte*, the events and the narration of events, the "objective as well as the subjective side" of history.[12] But we should also have to include, since the "advantages" of German are themselves plural, the twofold meanings [*doubles-sens*] that, even if they are not opposite meanings, nevertheless bear witness to the "speculative spirit": thus *Urteil*, judgment and original division (*Enc. I*, § 166; *SL*, 628—in spite of appearances, this play on the word does not correspond to its etymology); *Erinnerung*, memory and internalization,[13] which itself belongs to the process of *aufheben* (*Propeadeutic*, § 140); *Gesetz*, the law and positedness (*SL*, 502); *Meinen*, to opine and to make mine (*Enc. I*, § 20) (in Jena, Hegel was opposing *Meinen* and *Sein*); *Sein*, being that which is also the essence—*Wesen*—through its past participle: *gewesen* (*SL*, 398); *erklären*, to explain and to bring something to light (*Enc. III*, § 467); *begreifen*, to conceive and to grasp (to seize), to take something in hand (*SL*, 584–85) (the *begreifen* is thus always also a *fassen*, but the reverse is not true; *fassen* is indeed the "last word" of speculative apprehension); *das Sittliche* and *Sitte*, ethical life and "the general mode of conduct" or "customs."[14]—And, henceforth, it will be impossible not to take into account all sorts of polysemies, of reminders of the semantic affinities, or, on the contrary, of inventions of such affinities (thus, as we already see, there is no single principle for determining all items of the collection; in some way, anything that loosens meaning up is good . . .):

Hegel does not forget to link *wirklich*, the actual, to *wirken*, to produce an effect (*Enc. I*, § 153), or *Reflexion* to its optical meaning
(*SL*, 399); he also makes sure to recall that chance, *Zufall*, is that
which falls,[15] that the cause, *Ursache*, is "the original fact," *ur-
sprüngliche Sache*,[16] or to underline that through the kinship of
Gedächtnis and *Gedanke*, "the German language has etymologically
assigned memory (*Gedächtnis*) . . . the high position of direct kindred with thought (*Gedanke*)" (*Enc. III*, § 464). As he moves across
his text he exploits its good fortunes, explaining, for example, why
spirits [*geistig*] have been given an appropriate name (*Enc. II*, §
372) or how knowing "by rote" [*auswendig*] is to have extracted
from [*aus*] the inside of the I (*Enc. III*, § 462) or still how the
"naïve" [*unbefangen*] is the one that is "not caught" in reflection,[17]
whereas the "pondered" thought [*nüchterne* Denken] is also a
thought that has not broken its fast (*LHP*, 1:18). When it is no
longer possible to use these encounters as a basis for elaborating a
particular demonstration, it does not mean that discourse has to
prevent itself from making use, in passing, of their auxiliary resources: for example, one will bank on the play of the example (*Bei-
spiel*);[18] play with the thought of the *Meinen* that *meint* (*LHP*,
1:12); with *be-* and *ge-zwungen*, to be overcome and to be coerced;[19]
with *demonstration-monstration*, proof and exposition (*SL*, 630);
beweisen-weisen, to prove and to exhibit (*A*, 1:24); *Zeugen* and
zeigen, testimony and to prove oneself (*LHP*, 1:73); or else with
Qual and *Quelle*, which have been reinscribed elsewhere,[20] or else,
to suspend (provisionally) this proliferating enumeration at the
sound of the chimes: *Dinge-Denken*, things and thought sound together in language, and in any case in the text of the *Science of Logic*
that one comes across once again by chance: "things and the thinking of them—our language too expresses their kinship—are explicitly in full agreement [*übereinstimmen*], thinking in its immanent determinations and the true nature of things forming one and
the same content."[21]

Hegel indeed does not stint. No restriction comes to affect this prodigal economy of the polysemic and of the polyphonic; no definite operation comes to delimit the space or the regime of the property or properties of words. And it is becoming apparent that, if this space and this regime are not that of the *lexical stage* as such, polysemy is unlikely to regulate and to control its own deviation. It is rather called upon by an "a-semy," or else by *another* "semy," and polyphony by another voice.—But if chance here appears to reign, it is insofar as the chance at issue is, after all, not only that of chance encounters through the thread of a text; it is also the chance that presides over the meaning of words: the analysis of judgment in the *Science of Logic* opens up with the critique of the *names* "subject" and "predicate" and of the *names* that can appear as the "subjects" of a judgment, "God, spirit, nature, or whatever it may be" (*SL*, 624), since with names one is still in the "general idea [*Vorstellung*]" and "what is to be understood by a name" is "contingent and a historical fact [*Faktum*]" (*SL*, 625).[22]

Let us not forget, however, that we are here enumerating the speculative privileges of *German*: does Hegel's mother tongue somehow not elude chance, the factuality and the facticity of words (if the *names*, which have just been at issue, can have the value of paradigms of *words* in general), since it in fact possesses here and there—as if against the *Faktum*, of the crude fact—the effectivity of the speculative in the facts of language? Is Hegel not the one who exclaimed: "To speak in one's language is one of the highest moments of culture [*Bildungsmomente*]. A People is its own master. Out foreignness [*Fremdartigkeit*], including Latin literature [*Lettern*]!"[23]—And admittedly for Hegel, the privilege of the mother tongue is not an empty word, even though, as we saw, it is constantly submitted to the quirks of a prodigal fate, instead of being conferred, as it should be, by the law of blood [*par la loi ou par le sang*]. It is thus worth examining more closely these singular "privileges," that is, to analyze the exact nature of this maternal "wealth" that "delights" the speculative thinker. It turns out that it does not conform, as one could expect, to a theory of natural or original value[24]—and that generally speaking, as far as speculative language is concerned, nothing in fact functions one-sidedly.

It will suffice here to summarize the results of an analysis that could well be carried over to many other texts (and that could be the object of another work):

1. If the German language holds privileges, the appropriation of the science must nevertheless be done in each mother tongue. Had Hegel himself, by chance, had the privilege of doing so, he would have taught in a language other than German. Indeed, when he believed that he might go to Holland, where van Ghert was inviting him, he wrote to the latter: "With respect to the language in which lectures are normally given in Dutch universities, I would have, at first, to lecture in Latin; if customs allowed such a deviation from usage, I would soon seek to express myself in the language of the country, since in order genuinely to master a science, it is essential to do so in one's mother tongue."[25]—Speculative thought thus also speaks Dutch, and must, if need be, do so (namely, when the thinker is a professor, which in Hegel's case is not simply an accident).[26] *Any* language, therefore, is a mother tongue, and there is no mother language [*langue-mère*] or first language [*langue* princeps]. And if the mother tongue of the German has the privilege of a verbal originality that very often plunges into the origin [*Urteil, Ursache, Abgrund* . . .], it is not in turn to confer an originary nature to this language. The presence or the presentation of the origin in language, in *such* and *such* a language, and *for a German*, in German, is itself of a Babelian origin—which, of course, does not make much sense.

2. Whatever the importance and the number of privileges of German may be, the latter does not claim monopoly. It is not

alone in being able to produce "speculative meanings," and, in the text of *Natural Law*, which we recalled, the Greek *ēthos*, for example, says as much as the German *Sitte*. German, moreover, cannot provide for speculation's every needs: the texts of the *aufheben* themselves state it, even though always in somewhat confused and embarrassed formulas (but does the embarrassment itself not indicate that nothing here admits of a simple solution?). The preface continues beyond the point where we left it: "Philosophy therefore stands in no need of a special terminology; true, some words have to be taken from foreign languages but these have already acquired through usage the right of citizenship in the philosophical realm" (*SL*, 32).[27] And let us note that the "right of citizenship" is not naturalization, all the more since Hegel adds that "an affected purism [*ein affektierter Purismus*] would be most inappropriate where it was the distinctive meaning which was of decisive importance" (ibid.). The Thing, the thing-in-itself, the matter of thought contributes to babelize the privileged language.—And the Remark on the *aufheben* itself ends, as we saw, by this appended remark, itself somewhat embarrassed too: "We shall often [*noch öfter*—this can also mean: even more often] have occasion to notice [*Bemerkung*] that the technical language of philosophy [*Kunstsprache*] employs Latin terms for reflected determinations, either because the mother tongue has no words for them or if it has, as here, because its expression calls to mind [*erinnert*] more what is immediate, whereas the foreign language suggests more what is reflected" (*SL*, 107). The privilege of *aufheben*, then, concludes nothing. On the contrary, it opens up onto the frequency of the necessary borrowings from foreign languages. Better, it is "here" the case of such a borrowing: here, that is, where *aufheben* itself has needed another designation for its "more precise meaning [*Bestimmung*]." One appeals to *Moment*—as fitting, suitable, admissible . . . —a Latin term (and/or French) that has received the "right of citizenship" in German for "suggest[ing] more what is reflected," the latter indeed constitut-

ing the "more precise meaning" of the *aufgehobensein* as the result
of the *sich aufheben*. *Aufheben* therefore seemingly always risks
"calling to mind more what is immediate."²⁸ As we have already
mentioned, is the mother tongue not indeed always threatened by
"bad habits of reflection"? (*SL*, 98). *Reflexivity* is thus both an essential character of the thing [*la chose*] that speculative discourse
must state, or *present*, and a conduct or a necessary attitude in the
handling of words that this discourse needs—and especially for dis-
tancing itself from a certain "maternal" immediacy (and this, let us
recall, in spite of the fact that this immediacy is *also* the place of a
"naïvety" curiously able to speculate or, if you like [but Hegel *does
not say this*], to imitate speculation). Even in the mother tongue,
the privilege of a word cannot be absolute; the "speculative spirit"
paradoxically dissolves or warps the "purism" of its favorite language, and the speculative word—*aufheben*—can be uttered only
by multiplying, in its language *among others*, speculative words, no
doubt a barely admissible, involuntary plural but nevertheless an
inevitable proliferation.

3. The privilege of the mother tongue in fact still corresponds to another motif itself ambiguous because it simultaneously brings
philosophical language closer to "natural" speech *and* hands it over
to the imperfections and the hazards of natural languages. It is the
motif of the rejection of terminology. Mother tongues—or natural or popular languages—are above all opposed to technical language. We just read as much: "Philosophy . . . stands in no need of
a special terminology." *Terminologie* (it is a borrowed word in
German . . .) designates discourse made up of *Termini*, of technical terms. The scholastic discourse of philosophy (the one that
Kant, as we know, liked to reactivate) functions by means of *termini*, and especially the discourse of formal syllogistics, which
Hegelian dialectic refuses and sublates.²⁹ The *termini* are the
artificial words *and* the fixed, not sublated, differences of the sub-

ject and of the predicate (that is also, let us recall, the *names* most
opened to criticism). Speculative discourse therefore resolutely
moves away from *termini* in all its acceptations, or its figures. Yet
the privilege of the mother tongue is not absolute; its capacity is
limited, and from the text of the preface to the text of the Remark
a strange sliding substitutes to the proscribed *Terminologie* its translation in good German: a *philosophische Kunstsprache*, which one is
after all not able to avoid speaking, and that Hegel seems at least
to recognize as a fact. The right to do without *Terminologie* does
not entirely reduce the fact of the *Kunstsprache*, and even if it is spoken in German, it has to include, by an ironic necessity, a few Latin
terms.[30]

Philosophical language cannot quite avoid practicing what it challenges or denounces; but it does so in order to avoid something else
that it no less, if not more, denounces and that has already been indicated: namely, the danger of enclosing speculativity within the
univocal, within the unilaterality of a word (the word *unity*, for example). Not only, then, does one not get around the property of a
speculative language, but any language, whatever its "logical"
wealth, is here and there, through immediacy, naïvety, thoughtlessness, in danger of being univocal, of losing or forbidding the
aufheben. The presence of speculative words—of these cases of
Darstellung—remains exceptional. For this reason one should no
doubt all the more delight in them, but one cannot explain them,
and these welcome exceptions do not, in any case, constitute the
grounds of language [*raisons*]. The "forms of thought" may be
"stored" in language (one would still have to know the status of this
storage—*Niederlegen*—of this deposit and of this imprint . . .); language is *not*, for all that, *speculation*. Far from it.—One does not do
the owner's tour of the property; but rather, one is carried along,
aimlessly, in a plural play of languages that are disappropriated.
Consequently, it is not a coincidence if the *Moment* toward which

the "reflected" *aufheben* slides should not only be a metic in language but should also make use of a metaphor of sorts—even though Hegel introduces this figure by means of a neutral statement, which can appear both to show an identity and to make a comparison (which further complicates the displacement): "In the case of the lever, weight and distance from a point are called its mechanical *moments* on account of the sameness of their effect, in spite of the contrast otherwise between something real, such as weight, and something ideal,[31] such as a mere spatial determination, a line" (*SL*, 107). This may mean that the *aufheben* metaphorizes [*métaphorise*] in its *moments* the theory of the lever or else that the process of the *Aufheben* always involves a mechanics of the lever (indeed, that this process is always that of a mechanics of the lever).[32] (We shall soon have to consider what the fact that, in general, mechanics is at work in speculation can mean).

Whatever these hesitations and chiaroscuros may be (which at least prove that the time for starting to distinguish something of the *aufheben* should have come), it is at least certain that the operation or the matter of the *aufheben* is never that of a word, of a single word, and never that of the word for itself. *There is no verbal speculation;*[33] there are speculative word*s*. And this plural carries along another form of diversity, whose work and obstacles in the reading of the texts on the *aufheben* one should have begun to recognize for a while. These words, none of which are ever absolutely suitable for the presentation of the speculative, must be arranged, combined in a syntax or in syntaxes. Consequently, we "know," since we undertook the reading of Hegel, that the latter requires us to abandon the discourse of ordinary propositions or, more exactly, requires its *aufheben*. Consequently, it was necessary to note that before being noticeable, or before drawing attention to itself, the word *aufheben* had slipped, after the abandonment of all univocal words, into one of these long sentences with multiple reversals, which signals the most characteristic syntax of Hegelian discourse.

And if the lexical stage still offers us a "naïve" spectacle with respect to what is at work in this word, it is indeed in syntax that such a staging should be stripped of its naïvety (or of its artifice).

Do speculative words become legible, according to their speculativity, only in speculative syntax? And might the latter allow us finally to decipher the Remark? One cannot help but make a detour via these questions.

4

The Speculative Proposition

These Bits of Wood were covered on every Square
with Paper pasted on them; and on these Papers
were written all the Words of their Language in
their several Moods, Tenses, and Declensions, but
without any Order. The Professor then desired
me to observe, for he was going to set his Engine
at work. The Pupils at his Command took each of
them hold of an Iron Handle, whereof there were
Forty fixed round the Edges of the Frame; and
giving them a sudden Turn, the whole Disposition of the Words was entirely changed . . . and
the Professor shewed me several Volumes in large
Folio already collected, of broken Sentences,
which he intended to piece together; and out of
those rich Materials to give the World a compleat
Body of all Arts and Sciences. . . .

—J. Swift, *Gulliver's Travels*

It is obviously not a question of developing an extensive theory of Hegelian syntax. In the field entitled "the speculative proposition" we will content ourselves to pick out indispensable material so as to attempt answering the question that has just arisen around the *aufheben* and its lexicon. In order to do so it will suffice to reconstitute certain articulations of Hegelian discourse around the concepts of *proposition* [*Satz*], as the syntactic unity, and of *grammar* [*Grammatik*], as the order and the science of language in its syntax. We shall soon see, however, that whether it be for carrying out this reconstitution (which already implies that we did not find a thematic exposition of this topic in Hegel) or for establishing a lexicon of speculative words, the Hegelian text does not allow us to follow, in a straightforward manner, the thread of a discourse. Here again, the yet necessary speculative theory of syntax is dispersed and is disarticulated from text to text; it goes absent where one was expecting it, and it is brought out [*se met en relief*] in unpredictable contexts—never in the pure style of *theory*.

Everything here could in fact start (again) with the question or the exigency of another text, of another writing or another style, as though we had already come back to our point of departure, to the precondition of Hegelian exposition (which is, one suspects, neither only an assumption, nor even only an analogy).—Hegel wrote in 1805: "We no longer have so much to do with *thoughts*. We have enough of them, good and bad, beautiful and bold. Rather, we have to do with *concepts*. But in that thoughts are *through themselves* immediately made valid, whereas concepts on the contrary must be made comprehensible, the form [*Form*] of writing [*Schreibart*] thereby undergoes a change and acquires a form of appearance [*Aussehen*] demanding a perhaps painful effort, as with Plato and Aristotle."[1] Thoughts are themselves immediately made valid: the immediacy of words, especially in the mother tongue, is therefore no doubt suitable for them; but concepts require a change of writing, not so much in order to express or *prepresent* [*préprésenter*] them but rather for their very conceivability.—The difference from the concept to thought is not clarified, neither by means of a concept (in the ordinary logical sense of the term) nor by means of an image (as though Hegel were saying that the concept is to be grasped—*begreifen, fassen*—more than to be understood—*verstehen*). It is only marked in this way: *conceivability*, and even above all, the *being-concept* has to do with *form*. Nothing precise is said concerning this very form, apart from the example of the two great patriarchal figures of philosophy (with their books, a little as in Raphael's *The School of Athens* . . .)—that is to say, apart from the example of two writings as different from each other as they can be: on the one hand, Plato, whose qualities, indeed, whose literary researches are extolled by the entire tradition (Hegel does not miss the opportunity to do so in *Lectures on the History of Philosophy*), and, on the other, Aristotle (the one whose insight into the speculative concept Hegel so keenly celebrates), that is, lecture notes and reconstituted treatises (namely, one of the forms of Hegel's "work"). By analogy, then, with both at once, and at least insofar as reading both of them requires "a painful effort," the concept must let itself be conceived in (and perhaps *as*) a certain form of writing.—One can and must say that Hegel will subsequently abandon this program, which is in many ways romantic, at least as a determined and explicit one. But one can and must as well wonder whether Hegel might not have preserved it and somehow accomplished it (suffice it to recall once more the text that we read as a preamble). A question, as one sees, which takes the form of the *Aufhebung*—the *aufheben* of the program of writing and the writing of the *aufheben*: what strange relation, neither formally written nor rigorously sublated, can thus interlace these two motifs?

We shall not *reply* to the question: Hegelian discourse nowhere does so. But it is against it, along it or on its edge, that we shall see Hegelian discourse being laid out, used and scattered, to the very extent that it is forced to change its form, as if the means and the ends of its *thought* were displaced or were exceeded by themselves in the *transformation of form*, a way, for the discourse of the concept, of writing itself, of being the text—*Schreibart*—the means by which (as which) it becomes "conceivable," that is, it *presents* itself. Let us once again recall that it is, in any case, in a certain *Schreibart* of discourse that we saw the *aufheben* introduce, insinuate itself in the first paragraph that practiced the "great Hegelian style" in the midst of a text that had just brushed aside a few words and challenged the proposition in general.

It is from the latter that we must start off again. As we know, the condemnation of the proposition constitutes one of the most insistent, proliferating, and also most untimely themes (in view of the various contexts in which it appears) of speculative discourse. It is not a coincidence if, since the beginning of this work, we have already had to read at least two texts of such a condemnation (in the Preface to the *Phenomenology* and in the first chapter of the *Science of Logic*). There might be no Hegelian preface or introduction that does not bear the trace of this condemnation, which is then repeated in the body of the works, now with a well-determined logical function (in particular, concerning the theory of judgment), now at the slightest occasion (that is, concerning the conditions of exposition of any element of the system), as a restless [*inquiet*] and urgent reminder, as the very restlessness [*inquiétude*] of the speculative, seeking *to be heard* at the price of an extreme tension in its refusal of the proposition.

Hegel was already stating this refusal in 1805, in a form that can sum up all the others: "it is not good for philosophy to have a principle [*proposition*] and to be able to say: this *is* or is *nothing*."[2] It is thus not good but deplorable or dangerous for philosophy to affirm or to deny, in general to state anything concerning any subject at all—but, more particularly, or as the model and (the structure) of statements do, unilaterally to state *being* or *nothing*, and thus, *not to state the aufheben* concerning something [*au sujet de quelque chose*]. For it is, precisely, the *subject* as such, and what necessarily accompanies it, the predicate and the copula, in other words, the parts of discourse that, in the proposition, create an obstacle or a threat to philosophy. Their (unavoidable) determination as *parts of discourse* attaches to them, on the mode of a reciprocal unilaterality and exteriority, determinations whose (speculative) truth can yet only consist in the passage of the one into the other and in the annulment [*annulation*] of their difference. The annulment—the formation of a ring[3]—cannot therefore *be formed* elsewhere than in the *aufheben*, in an *aufheben* that sublates, jointly or, better, identically, the determinations of the thing and of parts of discourse. Or else—if sublation is actualized only insofar as it is expressed, as it *takes place* in the *Ausdruck*—in an *aufheben* that, for "being itself," that is, for not being nothing, but without being "being" . . . must in fact be the *aufheben* of the proposition: the *aufheben* of the proposition such as we already had to read it—and to give up reading it. And because the *Satz* simultaneously belongs to two registers, the logical and the grammatical ones, one has to follow the economy of the annulment on the two registers. But this raises at least three questions: how is the proposition annulled in logic? how is it annulled in grammar? and how is the difference between logic and grammar annulled (and, therefore, between the concept and syntax, or style)? Let us consider, at least as far as possible, these questions in order.

The logical *Satz* is the form of judgment.[4] The Hegelian logic of judgment corresponds right through to the annulment of this form. In this logic—at the end of an analysis that will have both underlined the word *Urteil*, as being a speculative word charged with originary meaning, and challenged the formalism of every statement of predication—it is admitted that "the subject and the predicate themselves are each of them the whole judgment" (*Enc. I*, § 180:256) and consequently, that the predicative statement, deprived of truth in that it connects two immobile determinations in exteriority, is resolved into each of its terms. This is the first annulment of the logical proposition. It is also its first *aufheben* since, henceforth, the judgment is sublated (or according to an already known process, *has already been sublated*) into a syllogism: "What has been posited in fact is the unity of the subject and the predicate as the Concept itself. The Concept is the fulfillment of the empty '*is*' of the copula; and since (as subject and predicate) its moments are at the same time distinct, the Concept is posited as their unity, as the relation mediating between them. [This is] *the Syllogism*" (ibid.).

Before going further let us note the word, the verb that gives rhythm to this sentence, that slips in at the decisive moment when one rises from the predicative form [*où l'on se relève*]: to posit—*set-*

zen. The *setzen* is, in particular, the first property of *reflection*, that is, of the gesture through which, in the *Science of Logic*, the general sublation of the immediate logic of being into a logic of essence is carried out: "[reflection] is . . . only as a returning movement, or as the negative of itself. Furthermore, this immediacy is the sublated negation and the sublated-into-self" (*SL*, 401). The truth of judgment is a positing: its negation and its sublation, the being-posited [*l'être-posé*] of its annulment, that is to say, of its identity turned over into each part of the proposition. The *Satz* is sublated into *setzen*, or, to coin a German verb, the *sätzen* is sublated into *setzen*. It is only just a matter of a vowel, of a nuance—*Schattierung*—or of an accent. This is where the *aufheben* of the proposition passes.

Aufheben passes in the syllogism, then—at least insofar as one has to translate the German *Schluss* according to its *terminological* value of syllogism, which does not limit its meanings to it (but which also first of all signifies the end, the conclusion and the inference in all senses of these terms. The traditional use of this term in German, instead of the scholastic one, somewhat eases the operations to which Hegel submits the concept.) And the dialectical economy of the syllogism in turn is adjusted to the two moments or the two sides of an *Aufhebung*. But the latter, as we shall see, might not be quite like the others.[5] It is indeed nothing less than the *aufheben* of the *form* (of judgment, of the *Satz*) into the *form of the rational* ("since any such import can only be rational in virtue of the determinacy that makes *thinking* into reason, it can only be rational in virtue of that form, which is the syllogism" [*Enc. I*, § 181:257])—in the other form or syntax that must be that of reason. The stakes of the syllogistics are to make the content of speculative rationality appear in its form and therefore to articulate speculative meaning. What is at issue is therefore nothing but *to annul the Aufhebung*—to make it come full circle, to *posit* it, by suppressing the erratic dispersion of its word, or to accomplish the return of all these returns of the *aufheben*, which, according to its Remark, "repeatedly occurs."

The syllogism is indeed the annulment—it is the first side of the *aufheben*, which is carried out in it: "[t]he actual is One, but it is equally the stepping asunder of the moments of the Concept; and the syllogism is the cycle of the mediation of its moments, the cycle [*Kreislauf*] through which it posits itself as One" (ibid.). The Hegelian syllogism is therefore at first the suppression of the formal syllogism of the understanding. The entire course of the Hegelian syllogistics consists in suppressing successively all the determinations attributed to the syllogism as such, at the term of which eventually for positing, as the sublated truth of the form of the rational, a syllogism without syntax and without figures—the *Schluss*, the conclusion, the end of all proposition. The outcome of the syllogism is indeed its own passage over into "the object," that is to say, the moment when, *in conformity with* the sublating law of speculative exposition, the form of the rational, far from being simply posited and delimited as the preliminary organon of the work of thought, it is sublated into its own content. A content that is nothing other than this form, insofar as to finish (itself) off, the latter has sublated itself. Completed, syllogistic syntax is presented as an object, without predication or consecution. The syllogism has thus become the object.

If the object, as the product of this passage, is put in relation with the Concept (which as far as its proper form is concerned has vanished in this transition), then the result may be *correctly* expressed by saying that the Concept . . . and the object are *in themselves the same*. But it is equally *correct* to say that they are *diverse*. Precisely because each statement is as correct as the other, each of them is as incorrect as the other; expressions of this kind are incapable of presenting [*darstellen*] the genuine relationship. (*Enc. I*, § 193:269)

What kind of expressions (*Ausdrucksweise*)? It is the affirmation (or the negation), the unilateral statement of a proposition. Once the syllogism is sublated, the proposition, with its undifferentiated correctness, still hinders the enunciation of the sublated syllogism. In the proposition—as far as meaning is concerned—it is right that the difference be suppressed, but as far as syntax, the propositional form itself, is concerned, it is no less right that it be preserved. The *Satz* therefore has exactly the same content or the same property as the *aufheben*; but it loses them immediately inasmuch as it *is* not the property of the unity that it states: there is not one but many propositions, and the proposition is "essentially" plural, articulated. The syllogism as such is precisely the articulation of propositions, therefore their exteriority, and it is as such that it has *aufgehoben* itself. The syntactic plurality annuls the annulment of the proposition, or rather, and because this second annulment is seemingly no longer dialectic, the syntactic plurality persists and insists, bothersome, insufficient, in spite of the annulment of the proposition. The life of the concept is sublated into a death without sentences, but how can one "present" this death "genuinely"?

Semantics is, in any case, here of no help. In the text there is no semantic relay or sublation of the propositional syntax. On quite the contrary, speculative words are absent, and far from invoking them, the text wears itself out only challenging the "triviality" of the proposition, *attracting notice* to it [*à la faire remarquer*], in a desperate gesture whose style suddenly surprises us: "As is always the case, the speculative identity is not the trivial one, that Concept and objectivity are in-themselves identical; this is a remark that has been repeated often enough, if the intention is to put an end to the stale and totally malicious misunderstandings about this identity. But, of course, there is no hope of achieving this at the level of the understanding" (*Enc. I*, § 193:270). If discourse momentarily loses its magisterial calmness, and if it makes a polemical deviation within the logical exposition, one must no doubt detect in it the trace of a certain *limit* to this discourse, which has indeed just been limited by exceeding itself, and which, should one not be favorable to it, cannot but have given all hope of being heard, of making this voice of the limit [*voix de limite*] heard—this voice at the limit that is henceforth its own. But it is definitely also because the *remark* that it *repeats* with exasperation, the remark on the radical difference between the speculative identity and the "trivial one" (such as a proposition can state it), has in fact already been inscribed for whoever knows how to read (for whoever knows how to hear: and this is also why the two motifs of the "deviation" of discourse, the polemical and the logical ones, finally merge).

It has been inscribed by and *in* the syllogism itself, that is, *in* the articulation of propositions, and as the second side of their *aufheben*. The syllogism—and its propositions—have really already produced the form where speculative truth is stated.—Hegel's silence or mood, in each of the texts where the sublation of the proposition is signaled—here as in the Preface to the *Phenomenology*—mark what Hegel *does not want* to say, whereas his entire discourse could (and at times appears to) want to say it: namely, that there might be *another* "expression" than that of propositions.

Another expression: this would then be a word or goodness knows what semantic purity or semantic absolute. But just as the proliferation of speculative words was carried along in syntax, syntax forbids the return and the recourse to the word. *Schluss*: it is the end of logic as far as its form is concerned; it is the *preservation* of the syllogism and, in it, of propositions. Hegel's logical syntax no longer passes over into its other or into another, and indeed, once the syllogism is posited, it will not pass. Rather, everything will pass through it. This conclusion of formal logic (of the part of the logic of the concept that corresponds to ancient logic—and that in fact keeps wrestling with the latter) determines the general form of the whole of the *Science of Logic* and of the *Encyclopedia* itself. In the latter it is in syllogisms that the entirety of the philosophy of nature is stated, and it is in an ultimate triplicity of syllogisms that the Idea, the speculative as such or, better perhaps, the speculation of the speculative, is accomplished. The "syllogism" is not a speculative word; it is an ordinary one—*Schluss*, which moreover functions here as a technical *term*; it designates a form, form; it designates the speculative in its form, in the only possible syntax of discourse, which is that of the proposition. The Hegelian *Schluss* simultaneously puts an end to all propositions and to all attempts to move away from the proposition. And Hegelian discourse, that is, the speculative proposition, is held (is articulated, is stated) exactly *from that place* [de ce lieu]. This is why, as we read in the Preface to the *Phenomenology*, "the philosophical proposition . . . *is* a proposition" (*PS*, 39); why "the *definition of the Absolute* from now on is that it is the syllogism. Expressed as a proposition this determination becomes: 'Everything is a syllogism'" (*Enc. I*, § 181:257). (And if, in the last sentence, the expression by means of a proposition appears, rather, to play the role of a concession, of a clarification given in a trivial language, hence of a substitute [*Ersatz*][6] with respect to the truth of the absolute that is at issue— one cannot help but recall that, at the same time, according to the terms of the *Phenomenology*, "the sublation of the form of the proposition . . . must find explicit expression. . . . This alone is the speculative *in act*" [*PS*, 39–40]. "Everything is a syllogism" would thus state the actuality of the absolute *in spite of* the propositional form that is used in it, but it *would be* this actuality *because* the proposition is expressed in it . . .).

The sublation of the proposition—or the nature of the speculative proposition—was what we were looking for in preamble, in order to read the *aufheben* in the text. One undoubtedly now sees better what one has yet never stopped seeing, in the chiaroscuro that shrouds these texts: namely, the extent to which the condition of reading is indeed the very condition of the concept and that of the text. There is nothing else to read but the text, and there is nothing else to do but to repeat this reading: everywhere, its propositions are philosophical propositions, and reciprocally, everywhere, the *aufheben* "repeatedly occurs." Never will such a perfect, exclusive closure have enclosed in itself the thickness of a volume, abolishing its entire outside. The *Aufheben* is not a concept whose intelligibility a demonstrative play of propositions might lead to; *aufheben* is to read propositions, to read a writing whose form "undergoes a change" and that requires, indeed, a "painful effort". . . .

. . . For there remains, precisely, the "modification of form," a modification—*Änderung*—an alteration of which we know nothing, and of which we know in any case nothing that is submitted to the form of knowledge without *aufheben* (or without alteration?). In seeking, in one way or another, to master this imperceptible modification, which activates the speculative proposition in (by means of which?) propositions, the *Satz* of the absolute in (as?) its *Ersatz*, in attempting to posit its concept, we shall first of all establish that the text of the *Science of Logic* disconcerts or thwarts the very principle of this research—which is not without causing some worries [*ce qui ne va pas sans inquiétude*]. In one of the Remarks of the first chapter, following the passage underlining the insufficiency of the proposition, which we already quoted, Hegel indeed writes:

To help express the speculative truth, the deficiency is made good [*ergänzen*] in the first place by adding the contrary proposition. . . . But thus there arises the further defect that these propositions are not connected, and therefore exhibit [*darstellen*] their content only in the form of an antinomy whereas their content refers to one and the same thing, and the determinations which are expressed in the two propositions are supposed to be in complete union—a union which can only be stated as an *unrest* [*Unruhe*] of *incompatibles*, as a *movement*. (*SL*, 91)[7]

The unsublatable equivocation of this text is double: on the one hand, its last sentence can indeed just as well point to the limitations of an expression by means of propositions, at best unable to surmount an anxious agitation of sorts (the end of the text pursues, in this case, the critique of Schelling, which underlies its beginning), as indicate the "true" and the "good" regime of speculative expression, which would then seem to be presented as an unrest [*inquiétude*] and as a movement.[8] In the latter case, once again, one must either identify the sublation of the proposition with this *Unruhe* (but the negative value of the *Unruhe* risks reducing drastically or limiting the sublation at issue) or (and because Hegel writes: "which can *only* be stated *as* . . .") consider that the *Unruhe* brushes aside or tacitly expulses the *aufheben*. At the place of sublation one would here seem to come the closest to what the Hegelian claim of a *style* might be, the claim of the restless style, of the permanent transformation and of the painful effort—of this style, indeed, that we momentarily thought to be able to call the Hegelian "grand style," the one that, a few lines later in the *Science of Logic*, will suddenly *make the aufheben pass* [*faire passer l'aufheben*]. (A style could then here mean: *neither* the statement of truth according to the laws of the statement *nor* some substitution [*suppléance*] of the speculative statement, if substitution should aggravate "the lack." Discourse would here neither be true nor take the place of truth.)—One sees that whatever the case, one would grasp—*fassen*—the *aufheben* only on condition of letting it vanish—*verschwinden*—and, consequently, one would grasp nothing of it. It undoubtedly does not mean that one can hope to grasp it elsewhere or otherwise. But it does not mean either that one must hurry to let the *aufheben* slip away, imagining that, cunningly or through a negative epiphany of sorts, this is how it is finally presented or that this is how one can identify the *aufheben* in the "movement" of Hegel's text. For this equivocal restless movement comes precisely to trouble its presence and its identity. One thus ought patiently to be confined, at least as far as possible, to these hesitations, these displacements, these deviations that accumulate from text to text. "Unrest" is neither the name nor the nickname of the *aufheben*: it makes it restless.

One cannot therefore master what pertains to the modification of form, but one cannot, on the other hand, avoid to be submitted to singular alterations. In the repetition of reading, a displacement or a confusion occurs between the statements of Hegelian logic, between all the occurrences of the *aufheben*. And this displacement may consist above all in the way in which the *aufheben* never occurs in the same way, is displaced from word to word, slides along from text to text, forbids us to accomplish the logic of the syllogism otherwise than by returning, albeit in equivocation and agitation, to the proposition—whose concept is, from then on, strangely confused, since one begins to fail to distinguish its relations to or its deviations from speculative truth. But in fact, it is the *aufheben* itself that gets its own concept entangled in even a stranger manner—as if, in search of the form of the speculative, of its own form, it were *deforming* itself. For must one *sublate* the proposition or *modify* it? Must one *suppress-and-preserve* it or *alter* it? Or else: might there be identity, but what a singular misrecognizable one, between the *aufheben* and alteration, that is, between two terms that no dialectical sublation can articulate together?

If questions become absurd or meaningless with respect to the concept of the *aufheben*—and to the speculative in general—the arrangements that the text(s) of the *Science of Logic* make are no less constraining. They are encompassed in the formula that states the result of the first *moment* of the syllogism, the one that sublates the qualitative syllogism into a syllogism of reflection. From this operation, Hegel writes, "With regard to the form a double result has now been established [*Hierdurch ist zunächst an der Form zustande gekommen*]" (*Enc. I*, § 189:251).[9]

"Right at the level of form," then, one leaves the formal syllogism, the "forms" and the "linkings" described by Aristotle but which Aristotle already did not let "encroach upon the speculative sphere" (*Enc. I*, § 187:263). And, with Aristotle and Hegel, one enters into the sphere where what the word *Schluss* designates will no longer have anything terminological or propositional about it. "Right at the level of form," this passage is accomplished without leaving the propositions, as a sliding [*glissement*] along them—the concept becomes conceivable "right at the level of form."

But where and how has this occurred?—Why ask? Has Hegel
not just written it? "Right at the level of form": it therefore occurs
[*cela s'effectue*]—or is conceived—everywhere, right through the
logical discourse, which, in its entirety, itself takes the form of the
syllogism. The passage "right at the level of form" takes place everywhere, as the *aufheben* does.—Everywhere, and therefore first of all,
precisely here, in this formula: *right at the level of form—an der
Form*. That is, just as much as the word *aufheben*, in a formula as
untranslatable from German into French as from German into
German or from French into French. What does "right at the
level" [*à même*] indeed mean? Surely not an identity, which nothing in the German phrase suggests. What does *an* mean? Next to,
by, very close to, nearby, along, to the brim or to the edge of. *An
der Form*: this does not amount to one concept (but to at least two,
if one could determine them: the concept of a *form* and that of its
edge, provided that the edge can be detached from it in order subsequently to be once again attached to it, and on the antinomic
condition that the difference from the edge to the form should
not be that of an outside from an inside, of a form from a content . . .).—*An der Form*: nor does this amount to a proposition.
Between the concept and the proposition, as between the form and
the edge, in this double in-between [*entre-deux*], through an economy of the interstice, of approximation, of the very small
difference, this does nothing other than *make us pass* logically to
what follows, that is, to the sublation of the syllogism. The syllogism—the form of the rational—is sublated and stands out against
a quasi identity of its form, on its own border, on the alteration of
a singular turn of writing—*Schreibart*—which attracts attention [*se
remarque*] insofar as, being written, it means almost nothing. The
aufheben of the proposition surely passes or occurs somewhere
[*passe ou se passe*]: precisely here, right at the level of this text that
is presented [*Darstellung*], in this formula whose presence is just as
well the vanishing of the concept as the irreversible alteration of the

proposition ("this *is* that" is transformed into "this occurs right at the level of that"). The modification of writing might be nothing else but, here and there in Hegel's text, a slight displacement, a loosening or a warping discreetly imparted to the predicative model. The proposition is modified in a preposition (would one dare say: right at the level of the preposition, itself posited or slipped into right at the level of the proposition?)—*an*, a little word that suffices to activate, to distend all the relations of strict inclusion or exclusion, all the determinations of copula. It is the *an* that carries away or carries along in the text the univocities of "being." And just as through the *aufheben* this *is* not that but this occurs right at this or that level, the *Aufheben* "itself" *is* not this or that but goes with(out) its meaning [*(se) passe (de) sa signification*] right at "itself." For, let us recall, the syntactic play of the *an* is also that of speculative semantics. The Remark writes: "It is a delight to speculative thought to find in the language words which have in themselves [*an ihnen selbst*] a speculative meaning" (*SL*, 107). The *an* here forms the mode of belonging of a meaning to a word, which is distinguished from the ordinary lexical meaning (or meanings).

Speculative meaning—the *aufheben*—and the speculative *aufheben* of propositions—in brief, if you like, the whole and appropriate determination of a "plastic" exposition of philosophy—is carried along thanks to the same preposition: *an*.[10] Even then it is wrong, or it would be saying too much, to suggest an identification of this *an* (even though it is through the *an* that the *aufheben* goes *without saying* . . .). This mode, this modification of writing—*Schreibart*—"is," if "being" is still at issue, or writes only what "slips through [one's] fingers," as it happens with all determinations: "Anyone who is not familiar with the determinations of subjectivity and objectivity, and who wants to hold fast to them in abstraction from one another, will find that these abstract determinations slip through his fingers [*durch die Finger laufen*] before he knows it, and that he says precisely the opposite of what he wanted to say" (*Enc. I*, Addition § 194:273). If *reading*—reading the text of the *aufheben*—is *fassen*, to grasp, one sees (one reads) that it is not "to hold tight" but to let slip or rather to familiarize oneself with a permanent fluidity, a permanent subtlety of all syntactic or semantic determinations, or else, with the subtlety thanks to which the semantics of the *aufheben* is reached only in a certain syntax, the syntax of the *an*, which inscribes nothing other than the *aufheben* of discourse (of propositions) right at the level of discourse. The logic of the *aufheben* turns out to conceal (but it conceals nothing: it is right at the level of the text, *an der Form*), among others, a subtle preposition (among others, for the *an* is not unique; it proliferates, in various forms, or right at the level of these forms, and without ever determining its *meaning* [*sens*], in all the textual slidings that we read, and whose calculation, it undoubtedly discreetly organizes).[11]

A preposition: would it then be a matter of grammar? Grammar is indeed still to be interrogated, if the latter well represents for Hegel, unlike the lexicon that pertains to the *material* of language, what concerns the *form* of language (*Enc. III*, Remark § 459). Could *an der Form* mean right at the level of grammar? And should the speculative truth of the dialectical process manifest itself as grammaticality? Undoubtedly: since this reading of Hegel has begun, we "know" that the *aufheben* entails a grammar, even if it is "other." Undoubtedly then—if at least it were possible to determine exactly what grammar's nature and regime are. And it is certainly not impossible to reconstitute, through the texts, a short treatise of Hegelian grammar (let us note, however, that it must be reconstituted, that it has no assigned place, and even, as we shall see, that it might in fact hinder the system . . .). But in carrying out this reconstitution, even if only very schematically, one quickly notices that something in the Hegelian grammar resists what one was looking for in it—the *aufheben*—or, if you like, that something in grammar resists Hegel.

Let us put it simply: the Hegelian grammar is confused, entangled, and shameful. It shows up (since it does show up, and, given the privileges of language [*du langage et de la langue*] it cannot but show up) in the texts, through untenable discursive and conceptual formations, always in fact inserted by Hegel as if in passing, offhandedly, such as, for example, the following one from the Remark of the *Encyclopedia*, which we just recalled: "as to the *formal* element, again, it is the work of analytic intellect which informs [*einbildet*] language with its categories: it is this logical instinct [*logische Instinkt*] which gives rise [*hervorbringen*] to grammar [*das Grammatische*]" (*Enc. III*, § 459:215). Let us leave aside the incredibly confused (and no doubt inextricable) system of these entries and exits, of these mixed entreaties whose logical mechanism remains undecidable. Let us note the major "concept": the grammatical is the work of a "logical instinct." This category is probably a hapax, in any case, a rarity in Hegel. One finds elsewhere more than one "instinct of reason" or "of the spirit," a teleological category wholly disposed toward the sublation of living nature. But as far as the logical is concerned, it is the human and the spiritual sublation of any nature. What is a "logical instinct"? Perhaps the very formula of this sublation. Which is probably not false. Grammar is very likely the *aufheben* of nature (of the mother, of the people) into spirit (language, syntax). Yet Hegel never says so. A "logical instinct" is also, is above all, a preliminary, inchoative form of logic, which, as such, can scarcely be delimited—something that is not expressly tied to logic by the bond of the *aufheben*. The "naïvety" that is, after all, the lot of language also affects grammar.

This is why the latter is in fact tied to logic by means—external or marginal—of the *Bildung*. It indeed belongs to the *Bildung*—to education and culture—that is, to the favored domain of the prefaces, of the texts that are outside the system or that are almost outside the system (everything is a matter of the "just about"), or else

to this category—"philosophical culture"—under whose heading
Hegel sometimes arranges every philosophy that precedes his
own.[12] The *Bildung* always has something to do with the empirical—as does grammar. The most developed text that Hegel has devoted to grammar is an empirical, occasional text, whose finality is
wholly a matter of *Bildung*: a School Address.[13] One hears in it that
"grammatical studies . . . form the beginning of logical culture" and
even "elementary philosophy"; one learns that "the grammatical
study of an *ancient* language" constitutes "a rational activity,"
which is opposed to the "thoughtless habit" in the usage of "the
mother tongue." But even so, grammar remains irrevocably external to the properly and strictly logical process, or, more exactly—
if it is possible here to hope for exactness—it belongs to the process
only on the mode of a relative exteriority, that is, on a mode that
for us (for us, readers and readers according to the speculative *for
us*) always remains partly illegible. Grammar is made for children;
its abstraction is suitable for their age; it is not yet genuine reading, for its abstractions "are in some way isolated letters [*Buch-
staben*], and more precisely the vowels of the spiritual [*geistig*],
with which one begins to spell out [*buchstabieren*] the latter, in
order subsequently to learn to read it."[14] Grammar is the literality
of the spirit, and one can (one must) well understand that, in the
text of the spirit, there will literally be nothing else but grammatical data—but, additionally, there will be—and this addition is indispensable—the good reading, ordinary reading, the reading that
gives the tone, the accent. In fact, there will be the consonant:
grammar, as we just read, is vocalic; it whispers, as Jacobi's vowel;
it does not articulate. Now, "the form of the proposition is the appearance of the determinate sense, or the accent that distinguishes
its fulfilment" (*PS*, 38). Grammar—the *formal* element of language—does not act *right at the level of form*; or else what happens,
right at the level of the form that it is, is not yet the logical and
speculative passage. What happens right at the level of grammar

does not happen without leaving a remainder, at least not clearly, not distinctly: between noise and articulated speech, grammar mumbles [*ânonne*]. And when one proceeds *an der Form*—to the reading of the plastic exposition—grammar is discarded. There is, strictly speaking, no *aufheben* of grammar nor, strictly speaking, *in* grammar.[15]

Grammar thus drags along—in Hegel as in the entire philosophical tradition[16]—the incurable empirical character of its Alexandrian beginnings: the science—or rather the technique—of letters, the science—or rather the practice—of texts. Yet it is not a coincidence if the empirical grammatical moment is the moment of *form*, which, to be truly considered and dealt with in the Remark on language (which belongs, in the *Encyclopedia*, to the chapter on imagination), would require that one "anticipate the standpoint of analytic understanding" (*Enc. III*, § 459:214), on the basis of which, once again, one would enter into the syllogism (cf. *Enc. III*, § 466 and § 467). Grammar belongs to the dialectical process but in an "anticipatory" mode, which will never be elucidated in itself, which will confusedly remain a *requirement*. Why not wait for the opportune moment for dealing with grammar instead of "anticipating" it (that is, wait for the *relevant* moment, as one says in Old French or in German)? But the system has in fact always already "guessed" that this moment would not come.

Grammar can indeed only "enter" into (we shall see that this "entry" is but a way of slipping) the dialectical process from the bottom—if one dare say so—in the position of the moment that is most exterior to the spirit, to the spirit *tout court* and to the speculative spirit of language, or in a position that could be said, so as to underline its simultaneous dialectical and nondialectical nature, to be of excessive exteriority. In a word: grammar is *mechanical*. Grammatical mechanism, mechanics in language in general, is what explains—albeit obscurely—the confusion of Hegelian grammar. It puts the latter to work in an *aufheben* whose functioning it immediately blocks. In the 1809 School Address, Hegel declares that

> ... the mechanical side of the study of language is more than a necessary evil. For the mechanical is that which is foreign to the spirit, whose interest tends to digest [*verdauen*] the non-digested [*Unverdaute*] which has been introduced into it, to comprise [*verständigen*] what in it is still lifeless, and to appropriate it.—This mechanical moment [*Moment*] of the study of languages is in fact at once attached to *Grammatical studies* [*das grammatische Studium*].[17]

Grammatical mechanics is thus a *moment* and, consequently, an *aufgehobene*. The situation remains nevertheless confused on many accounts: first of all, the mention of the grammatical *moment* only appears in a marginal text, outside the system [*hors-système*], a discourse of *Bildung*. We then saw in what singular metaphorical chaos this sentence moves, going so far as to digest machines: a certain embarrassment, an engorgement of style here corresponds to an undoubted embarrassment of dialectics. It looks as though, at its height, that is also to say, at its most necessary moment (*aufheben* of the "foreign" and of the spirit), the dialectic of language was exceeding itself or as though, in language, dialectic was experiencing an excessive moment, a passage through absolute strangeness, a passage irremediably divided—not sublated—between the resumption of the *aufheben* and the immobilization of a mechanics. This is at least what we note if we examine more closely this mechanics; we see that somehow marked insistently by the accidents, the confusions, and the silences of the calculating machine of the Hegelian text, grammar will not recover from it [*ne s'en relèvera pas*].

One of these accidents—or one of these confusions—occurs precisely here, where we read that grammar is the *mechanical moment*. For the *Moment*, this "suitable" denomination of the reflected *aufheben*, is itself nothing but the name of a mechanism, or of an element of a mechanism—and we saw how ambiguously this mechanism came to function in the Remark on the *aufheben*:

without allowing us to decide absolutely between the metaphorical borrowing or the sliding of identity [*glissement d'identité*]. The meaning of *Moment* has not been sublated from its mechanical status: in one way or another, it is rather the lever "itself," which carries out, in the mechanics of its moments, the dialectical sublation. This might quickly throw us down into the unexpected accuracy of a singular literality: the lever sublates—and, as a consequence, there is a speculative machine. *Contradictio in adjecto* and nondialectical contradiction. Something here does not work properly, does not go down well [*ne passe pas*]. Could the excess or the mechanical (grammatical) block precisely intervene through the lever, in the very text of the *aufheben*? Could the lever, instead of lifting up [*soulever*]—and still less sublating—anything at all, function, unsettled, wholly otherwise, as a blockage?

> (*that is, as far as the mechanical constraints of composition are concerned, in printing terms: blockage: letters which are turned upside down, and which are provisionally employed to stand for missing letters [Littré]. Now, printing is a mechanical invention [at the service] of a sublation:* "[the newly invented Art of Printing] . . . *supplied the desideratum of the age in which it was invented, by tending to enable men to stand in an* ideal *connection with each other*" [our emphasis; Hegel, *Philosophy of History*]. *It is true that, just like grammar, this invention has already been held up somewhere in history: among the Chinese; for the latter* "continue to engrave the letters in wooden blocks and then print them off: they know nothing of movable types" [ibid.].)

Mechanics is indeed always more or less and only ever so slightly outdone in the dialectical process. Once it is *annulled* in the syllo-

gism, the concept becomes object—a "strange" [*fremdartig*] passage
that the syntax of propositions would not know how to express,[18]
an object whose first moment is the mechanism. "This is what constitutes the character of *mechanism*, namely, that whatever relation
obtains between the things combined, this relation is one *extrane-
ous* to them . . . [and] it remains nothing more than *composition*
[*Zusammensetzung*], *mixture* [*Vermischung*], *aggregation* [*Haufen*]
and the like. *Spiritual* mechanism also, like *material*, consists in
this, that the things related in the spirit remain external to one another and to spirit itself" (*SL*, 711). The mechanism accumulates in
it all the features of what one could be tempted to call a counter-
or a non-*aufheben*, if it were not more accurate, that is, here, more
disconcerting, to see in it a *block* in every sense of the word. If
grammar is mechanical, a certain form and a certain formation of
logic consequently turn out to take on the position of blockage in
it. But there is more: given the singular network of a permanent exchange between language and mechanics in Hegel's text, the accident aggravates its effects, the confusion spreads.

   If the mechanism is a moment in language, a certain usage of
language, on the other hand, is a paradigm of the mechanism, and
of the most mechanical mechanism, if one dare say so, of the *formal* mechanism: "Just as pressure and impact are mechanical relationships, so we have mechanical knowledge, too: we know things
by rote, inasmuch as the words remain without meaning for us and
are external to sense, representation and thought" (*Enc. I*, §
195:274).

The Remark of § 195 of the *Encyclopedia* is not only unusual in its
context (the chapter on mechanism): it both prepares and contra-
dicts the moment of the *aufheben* of language in thought (§ 463 to
§ 465). For this moment will be that of the suppression of meaning through the "recitation by heart," that is, through the "mechanical memory"; the latter constitutes "the passage into the func-

tion of *thought*, which no longer has a *meaning*" (*Enc. I*, § 464:223). The memory machine, the machine that empties words out of their meaning, leads us into the element of thought—into this "pure element" in which Hegel continually repeats that actual speculation can alone be produced and articulated in it. In order to have access to this element, discourse must jam when being recited. Recited language is a paradigm of the mechanism—it might be *the* paradigm of it—because in the dialectical process the mechanism might have no other function than that of blocking discourse on this emptiness *at the level of its form* [*à même sa forme*].— Henceforth, in the passage through which the whole of discourse is sublated in thought, "sublation" itself goes through the machine: no longer to have any meaning is, for *aufheben*, no longer to have *two* lexical meanings but rather only a speculative one.

Speculative meaning [*signification*]—which amounts to both the "meaning" of the word *aufheben* and the product of the process of *aufheben*—is thus that which has *no meaning*: neither, however, on the negative mode of the *nonsensical* (which would be unilateral) nor on the mode of a sublated meaning (in spite of the expression "speculative meaning")—for the machine has not sublated meaning but has exhausted it. Working at the level of form, it has suppressed meaning and preserved the empty word, thus passing itself for an *aufheben* but "of course" at the price of an inadmissible displacement of the *aufheben* (the mechanical operation would be an *Aufhebung* only on condition that the word and its meaning be rigorously considered *as being the same thing*, which, given the Hegelian "socratylism" that we had to mention, takes place, at the most, only for speculative words but at the price of extreme reservations and distortions: either this meaning is "naïve," or else it is not a meaning). There is no *aufheben* in a *sublated sense* [*en un sens relevé*]; there is only an *aufheben*, recited here and there in the text, that has no meaning, that does not have *meaning*—or that meaning does not have.—One goes through it by means of the memory machine, of the memory whose name, Hegel quickly notes, is itself a speculative word: "The German language has etymologically assigned memory [*Gedächtnis*], of which it has become a foregone conclusion to speak contemptuously, the high position of direct kindred with thought [*Gedanke*]" (*Enc. III*, § 424:223). But this passage through the machine with a speculative name, that is, "its organic interconnection with thought is one of the hardest points, and hitherto one quite unregarded in the theory of mind" (ibid.). —Hard (*schwer*, heavy . . .), indeed, given that the explanation one should at least partly expect (but for that, one must *return* to the moment of the mechanism, to the Addition to § 195), the explanation of memory by means of the nature of memory, by means of the machine itself, is forbidden without further ado:

Even in the domain of the spiritual world, mechanism has its place, though again it is only a subordinate one. It is quite right to speak of "mechanical" memory, and of all manner of "mechanical" activities, such as reading, writing, and playing music, for example. As for memory specifically, we may note, in this connection, that a mechanical mode of behaviour belongs even to its essence. . . . Nevertheless, anyone who has recourse to mechanics in order to explain the nature of memory and wants to apply its laws without further ado to the soul will thereby show himself to be a bad psychologist.[19]

The passage to speculative meaning—sublation, which, right at the level of the word [*à même le mot*], takes place in *aufheben* and in the sublation *of the* opposite meanings of *aufheben*—works by means of a machine *that escapes the laws of mechanics but knows no other ones*. In this sense, memory repeats the singular properties of the lever. Neither the one nor the other is the engineer's machine, but they are not the life of meaning either. They are rather "mechanics" [*des mécaniques*] in the old sense of the word, which designates uncultivated, illiterate, indeed, stupid or cretinous men, in whom one would find again a certain "naïvety" of language. One would have to coin for them the odd concept of a *naïve machine*—

yet a machine that can moreover be identified only by its speculative name: *Gedächtnis, whose speculativity is itself borrowed from some spring, mechanics, or machinery of language.*

Between grammar and memory, right at the level of form, language is reduced to mechanism. Mechanism resists the *aufheben*—and vice versa. The one or the other is uncalled for. Confusedly and paradoxically, it looks as though, in the Remark on the *Aufheben*, a discreet but powerful and paralyzing tension were taking apart the two poles and the two names of sublation, the speculative and the mechanical, the language and the lever, the *aufheben* and the *Moment*. The naïve machine is not a discursive apparatus that would ensure, by means of *regulated* propositions, the articulation of the *aufheben*; it rather disarticulates it; and because it is not learned, it is in fact scarcely a machine: it is rather an incomplete and exhausted mechanism, only half functioning or functioning in fits and starts, *blocking discourse in a hardly endurable tension.*

What can resolve—or break—this tension is the word, and particularly the name, to which the whole of this discourse will have already irresistibly brought us back a few pages ago. Only the name can escape the machine or set it going again (which, strangely, might come to the same in Hegel—strangely, that is, in such a way that a single "word" could "say" something about it: for example, the *escapement*, which is a regulatory mechanism . . .). Words and not syntax form the content of the *Hersagen*, of mechanical recitation: "one attaches no meaning to the words" (*Enc. III*, § 465:222). In the dislocated proposition, the disconnected parts of discourse, everything occurs as in the most elementary grammar: one "spells out the spirit"—and it is then that one is sublated [*c'est alors qu'on se relève*]; to spell out is to read; to recite is to think. But then the words that one pronounces are empty, without ceasing to be words.[20] They have no meaning, and good reading does not consist in giving tone. On the contrary, it forms the vanishing of the accent around which, as we have been noting for some time, everything here had to be played out. "The recitation of what has been thus got by heart is therefore of course [spontaneously—*von selbst*] accentless [*akzentlos*]" (ibid.). The word does not escape the machine in order to restore the semantic outside the syntactic, in order to draw out the purity of an onomastics or even of a speculative eponymy—there is no verbal speculation; the mechanism of *escapement* produces a word without accent, a word whose machine has worn out the accent.

The *aufheben* does not take place "in" the proposition but right *at the level of its form*, as the loss of accent, that is, as a pure *metrics*:[21]

This conflict between the general form of a proposition and the unity of the Concept which destroys it is similar to the conflict that occurs in rhythm between metre and accent. Rhythm results from the floating centre and the unification of the two. So, too, in the philosophical proposition the identification of the Subject and Predicate is not meant to destroy the difference between them, which the form of the proposition expresses; their unity, rather, is meant to emerge as a harmony. The form of the proposition is the appearance of the determinate sense, or the accent that distinguishes its fulfilment; but that the predicate expresses the Substance, and that the Subject itself falls into the universal, this is the *unity* in which the accent dies away. (*PS*, 38)

This text precedes, by one paragraph, the one stating that the plastic reading-writing must sublate the form of the proposition—the text that, from the outset, has forbidden us to grasp directly the *aufheben* in Hegelian discourse. The *aufheben* of syntax—that is, *the* syntax (the "exhibition") of the *aufheben*—has thus already been determined as a *zerstören*, a destruction. Not so much to the benefit of a meaning but rather of a meter—*Metrum*, a Latin word transcribed as such—which subsists alone when the accent has been extinguished or which, as recitation, *goes without saying*, without accent [va de soi *sans accent*]. The *aufheben* goes without saying, without accent—syllogistics, the form of the rational, is regulated by itself in metrics. Sublation is not a rhythm, "a swinging back and forth" between two terms or two poles in turn accentuated. It is, if it "is," meter without poetry, the mechanism without an accomplished machine, discourse without accent. Hence, its word has slipped among words and as if on the side or in the course of propositions so as to state [*articuler*] what neither syntax nor meaning can say. This word—*aufheben*—is stated in the accentless meter or is uttered by itself without accent.

Here is how the text of the *Aufheben* reads: in a metrical, mechanical way, right at the level of its form, in a neutral voice, by speaking in water—"Water, being without cohesion, makes no sound, and its movement, as merely *external* friction of its freely displaceable parts, yields only a murmuring sound [*Rauschen*]" (*Enc. II*, Remark § 300:137).

(A Voice of the aufheben?—"I propose, without emotion, to declaim the cold and serious strophe which you are about to hear. . . . Nevertheless be, if you can, as calm as I in reading these lines which I already regret offering you. . . .

Old ocean, crystal waved . . .

Old ocean, you are the symbol of identity.)[22]

5

The Word, the Speculative

> *Unity* and *difference* give out in a poor and mediocre sound, for example, against the splendour of the sun, against the East and the West, this fact that each thing has in itself its East and its West. But the gospel will be preached to the poor and they will see God.
>
> —Hegel, "Aphorisms from Hegel's Wastebook"

(It goes without saying that should we be able to conclude—schliessen—it would by now be done. But it would be the wrong move [le coup serait mal calculé]. The neutral voice does not have "a poor and mediocre sound." Dazzling, rather, it still announces the Good News [la bonne parole].)

Aufheben: the word that is pronounced without accent is nevertheless neither an empty syllable nor a humming from before the voice. Let us in fact reread, in a more neutral tone, suitable to reading, and particularly to the reading of a remark: "*To sublate*, and the *sublated* (that which exists ideally as a moment), constitute one of the most important concepts [*Begriff*] in philosophy. It is a fundamental determination which repeatedly occurs [purely and simply] throughout the whole of philosophy, the meaning of which is to be clearly grasped and especially distinguished from *nothing*. What is sublated . . . has . . . *in itself* the *determinateness from which it originates.*" And later: "The more precise meaning and expression which being and nothing receive, now that they are *moments* . . ." (*SL*, 107). If all the movement—or the movements—of the body of the Remark are made to erase or to muddle up the determination of meaning, the latter nevertheless constitutes the beginning and the end of it. *Aufheben* is not a word beyond words; it is neither an absence of meaning [*un néant de sens*] nor the unpronounceable name of a divine power. It has determinateness *right at itself* [*à même soi*]—*an sich*—that is to say that it has what the proposition proposes *right at itself*, without syntax.

It does not, therefore, keep itself in the background. Rather, if one dare say so, it *forms* syntax alone. It forms it by being pronounced in a determinate manner. It is pronounced, from moment to moment, as it is written in the text of the philosophy book and as it can be read. It is henceforth thrown into an exceptional relief. A *relief* is not an accent: it is a distinction and a remnant [*une éminence et un reste*]—a twofold meaning that, as we see, has nothing speculative about it (owing to its Latin etymology as to the use that we are making of it, the *relief* is the doublet, or the nondialectical double of *sublation*).[1]—*Aufheben* and all the speculative words, this is what remains, when, *right at the level of form*, and through the *relief* of the *an* [*par le relief d'un* an], form and its accent have disappeared. And what therefore juts out—the crests of the waves on the rustling water—is both, each time, the dispersed plural of speculative word*s*, and *the* word as such, the remarkable word ("*aufheben*" or another—but still *aufheben*), the word that is speculative but is so without syntax, without copula: the word, the speculative (or to be more precise "the word, comma, the speculative," or perhaps still in the propositional form: the word comma the speculative, since *virguler* is a verb, the act of marking the comma, the smallest of the pauses. In the speculative there is, in excess or at an angle, a comma, a small stick, a small verge).² It is with the relief of the word that we should be concerned—or, more precisely, with a series of discontinuous, subdued, or uneven reliefs.

The entire series will in any case be caught between what remains of the word in relief at the beginning and at the end of the *Science of Logic*, without being completed, and without its *reason* being calculable. (That is, between two determinations, following a movement or a *schema* that might be repeating very precisely that of the Remark: the latter goes from the determination of the meaning of a concept to the position of the determinatedness of *Dasein*, and we will easily see what correspondences—at least—can be established between these extremities and that of the *Science of Logic*. The latter is, as we know, a *"circle of circles"* [*SL*, 842]: the smallest of these circles—the innermost one, as it were—might then be that of the Remark on the *aufheben*, and this appended text thus forms the abyss of the text.)³ The *Science of Logic* has indeed begun with the "empty word," with the emptiness of the word as the immediacy of being. It ends by presenting itself as the presentation of the disappearance of the word: "logic exhibits the self-movement [*die Selbstbewegung*] of the absolute Idea only as the original *word*, which is an *outwardizing* or utterance [*Äusserung*], but an utterance that in being [*indem sie ist*] has immediately vanished again [*verschwinden*] as something outer [*Äusseres*]" (*SL*, 825).—No doubt, what is here stated under the heading of a limitation (*nur*) of the *Logic* corresponds to the position of *moment*, which is that of the *Logic* itself; the latter must indeed be sublated in the system, of which after all it constitutes only the form. But the logical moment—precisely because it is the moment of form, and because the form of this form, that of the syllogism, will not "pass over"—is also that of the sublation of all the other moments. Hegel has just written: "The *logical* aspect of the absolute Idea may also be called a *mode* [*Weise*] of it; but whereas *mode* signifies [*bezeichnet*] a *partic-*

ular kind, a *determinateness* of form, the logical aspect, on the contrary, is the universal [*allgemein*] mode in which all particular modes are sublated and enfolded [*eingehüllt*]" (*SL*, 824–25). The vanishing of the exteriority of the word is both the passage through the definitive and universal form (*with an extra word*)—and the vanishing moment, at whose extremity the word, in a new exteriority, or in its preserved and renewed exteriority, reemerges (*still another word, an extra word*). This reemergence or this resurrection (for everything here brings into play the example of the Word incarnate, dead and resuscitated, but without too much attention being paid to it and by playing on the ambiguity of the word: *das Wort*) is none other than that of the "empty word" with which we had to "begin." Such is the general relief of the *Science of Logic*, that is, the general relief of the entire system:[4] the vanishing of the word, which is also its exteriorization, its pronunciation. *Verschwinden, verklingen*: the accent that expires *still yields a sound—already* yields a sound, the first one, that of the empty word. Everything is finally placed in the hands of the mechanics of memory that recites; everything begins because, for a long time, from the end, memory has already recited the word.

Which word? all the words—so long as their accent vanishes. Not the Word then—a unique meaning and a unique accent—but a plurality dispersed through language or languages. Recitation is not the retention of a primitive word but the annulment of language as that which might be endowed with meaning and accent. And, for example, let us recall that right before the *Science of Logic* began, German language was reciting this meaningless(-ful) nursery rhyme: "Dinge-Denken." But this "before-after" of all the words always has the form, or always takes place right at the level of the form, of one word: *aufheben*. The relief is *aufheben*, the remarkable word, which repeatedly occurs for proffering everywhere the vanishing of the lexicon, of the lexical staging of (opposite) meanings. Hence, the form that the relief, the remarkable, takes, in its advent and its event, is always, repeatedly, that of the Remark on the *aufheben*: the happy surprise: "It is a delight to speculative thought to find that a language has come to use one and the same word for two opposite *meanings* of this word" (*SL*, 107). But that is also why the relief is plural, why it takes the form of an archipelago; for the happy surprise concerns word*s*, and hence Hegel quickly adds: "the German language has a number of such" (ibid.). There is no word that sublates within itself the whole of language; there is in language, or there remains in language,[5] many words in relief.—And if all of them, in their event as much as in their speculativity, take the form of an *aufheben*, the *word aufheben* is not for all that inordinately privileged,[6] as we already know: the immediacy and the thoughtlessness of the mother tongue threaten it; it goes through the *Moment*—that is, more or less, through Latin, the Latin whose *tollere*, however, "does not go as far as" the *aufheben*.

Syntax will thus have referred us back to semantics, to an incomplete, unfinished semantics (and semanticism) that works badly. Sometimes words are outdone [*en reste*]; sometimes they remain words. The happy surprise of speculative meaning in certain words does not yet allow us to state that "the word is speculative"; this proposition must be destroyed and sublated like the others; it is thus impossible to utter *the* unique word of the speculative. *Aufheben* is no doubt a good word,[7] but it is not the last word. One can only write, between syntax and semantics: *the word, the speculative*. For the singular regime of such a statement—if it can still be called in this way—might be none other than the one of the whole text of the Remark: the latter, indeed, can be neither summed up in the *meaning* of a word (in a "concept," of which we will never know if it announces or recalls it: it probably does both, and it annuls the construction of the concept) nor reconstituted in a rigorous logic (but only read as a singular aggregate or a passage from text to text).

This regime of reliefs (or, this area of reliefs) no doubt precisely forms what, in Hegel, ensures the constitution and the use of words. Without undertaking a comprehensive analysis of it, let us here briefly note some of its most salient elements:

The Relief of Phantasie

The Hegelian theory of the sign depends, as we know, on the moment of imagination (*Einbildungskraft*). Determined as a producer of signs, imagination is called *Phantasie* (as far as language is concerned, let us say that what is at issue is imagination in its least technicotheoretical [terminological] value, in its most active and free value)—as far as Hegelian determinations are concerned, *Phantasie* appeared as "symbolic, allegoric, or poetical imagination [*dichtende*: it is the literary, poetic composition of fiction]" (*Enc. III*, § 456:209). It is thus, in the third moment of imagination, *Zeichen machende Phantasie*, productive imagination creating signs, creating one or some sign(s) (ibid., § 457:211).—Words are thus made—*gemacht*—composed—*gedichtet*—by productive imagination. Now, productive imagination is an *Aufhebung*, the *Aufhebung* of the inside and of the outside, and more precisely, of the "proper" and of what one finds (outside, by chance, as speculative words): "Productive imagination is the centre [*der Mittelpunkt*; the middle, the middle term, and the means (*moyen*), for example, the means which the lever is], in which the universal and being, one's own [*le propre, das Eigene*] and what is picked up [*l'être-trouvé, das Gefundensein*], internal and external, are completely welded into one [*in Eins*]."[8]

Aufhebung, productive imagination, is reason: "Imagination, when regarded as the agency of this unification, is reason"—but "only a nominal reason, because the matter or theme [*Gehalt*] it embodies is to imagination *qua* imagination a matter of indifference [*gleichgültig*]; whilst reason *qua* reason also insists upon the *truth* of its content [*Inhalt*]" (ibid.).—One cannot say more clearly that the rationality of productive imagination is rationality itself, which operates on and in the word *aufheben*. Formal indeed, it is at least first of all of the general order of *logical* reason. It is thus indifferent to the content, or more precisely—and if we limit ourselves to the text, to the proximity of *Gehalt* and *Inhalt*, and to the sliding from the one to the other, which must have a speculative character in Hegelian language—it is indifferent to the *import* [*teneur*] of the content—*Gehalt*, the proportion, the share, the percentage—and, consequently, to the value, that is, as far as a sign is concerned, to meaning in its *determinateness*. The *lexical* import [*teneur*], for example, the division or the proportion of "two opposite meanings" in the same word—which, incidentally, is "improbable"—is indifferent. *Productive imagination* does not govern the lexical stage; it proceeds this side of it or elsewhere. And because the text does not here exclude that indifference to import [*teneur*] be just as well the nondifference (the nondetermination) of the *content* [*contenu*], a certain identity of form and content in productive imagination may well be equivalent (*gleichgültig*) to the "speculative meaning" that can be found "right at the level of" certain words—right at the level of these words upon which one comes by chance and which productive imagination sublates in order to unite them to speculative interiority without "claims" to meaning.

If such is the case, the theory of the sign opens up with the already sublated and sublating position of meaning (determined, but what on earth could a nondetermined "meaning" be?) in or through productive imagination—and the operation of productive imagination is itself less an *Aufhebung* (the subsumption under this concept of nature or of the structure of *Phantasie*), than it is, by means of a discreet connection between texts, from Remark to Remark, the very encounter with the word *aufheben*, of all the speculative words, or of the word, of the speculative—found, condensed, sublated, and thus making a sign or making signs.

This gives rise to a twofold relief: for the text on productive imagination keeps silent about the *aufheben,* or about any speculative word, which, moreover, is logical to do, since at this stage the order of words still remains to be produced.—But conversely, the Remark on the *aufheben* keeps silent on productive imagination, or at least, on this sort of productive imagination, which could, right at the level of certain words, be making a speculative sign or speculative signs. In other words, at the time of the Remark, the "delight" of the speculative thinker is not related to any determined faculty or activity of this "theoretical spirit" to which productive imagination and, consequently, the constitution of language belong.[9] This Remark without productive imagination does not therefore pertain to a sign but rather to a word without lexical notation, without semiology, to a word, *so to speak,* altogether suited in language and yet meaningless.—What is thus yet missing from the Remark for grasping (*auffassen*) the "meaning" that, in spite of everything, one has to grasp "in a more particular" way is indeed the determination of the agency, of the faculty or of the activity that allows the find, the *grasp,* and the delight. Insofar as what is at issue is after all a word, we might just have learned its name: it is productive imagination in or of speculative thought. And perhaps, if speculative thought takes shape in language, or fortunately comes upon its *own* means of expression in language, we might also be learning that it is productive imagination that does the *Darstellung* of speculative thought. Just as, in turn (or in advance), one must attribute to productive imagination a speculative meaning, which allows it to sublate, in a being-found [*être-trouvé*], the find that will unite the inside and the outside.[10]— But this is not spelled out. On the contrary, the *phantasiology* is missing from the establishment of the function and of the concept of the *aufheben*—of such an important philosophical concept; the word *aufheben,* as a word, inasmuch as it is, all the same, available in the order of signs (even if it exceeds or exhausts it), is all that remains of it, and the *relief* (the remnant) of this word is its *Phantasie*—a strange and unnamed *spekulative Phantasie.*

The Figure in Relief

As the Hegelian discourse on signs and on language unfolds, it will continually be supported—at least on one of its axes, the most properly or the least improperly semiological—by the very classical motif of the expressive exteriority of language and, therefore, of its conventional character. *Phantasie* proceeds by arbitrary decrees: but just as we were led to evoke Hegel's "socratylism," it is now important to examine more closely the Hegelian avatars of this motif.

In the *Aesthetics*, when Hegel introduces the "symbolic form of art," he begins by recalling, as a *register* anterior and exterior to that of the artistic symbol, the register of the "mere sign [*blosse Bezeichnung*]," which is defined by the "indifference [*Gleichgültigkeit*] between meaning and its expression" (*A*, 1:304).[11] In its usage, which could be described as merely semiological (since here the order of presentation of the sign and of the symbol is inverted with respect to the *Encyclopedia*), language is given over to the arbitrariness of this "indifference," that is to say, to empiricism, to this empiricism of meaning that is the lot of "naïve" (*Enc. I*, § 26) thought under the species of dogmatic metaphysics: the exactness of the *representation* can only be ascertained empirically, according to usage (that is, according to the lexicon and to grammar), *in* a word.[12]

The language of philosophy, however, will not be another language. It will not be a *Terminologie*, even though, already, the empiricism of meaning may oblige it—when it does not have the good fortune to fall upon a bon mot in language, or when the latter remains too immediate—to be practiced as a *Kunstsprache* and to borrow "quite often" from foreign languages. But whether it be a question of borrowing or of having the good fortune to come upon, philosophy possesses, with respect to the arbitrary convention of representation, a right that defines its own usage of language (such a *usage* being what irremediably replaces, for example, the Leibnizian idea of the constitution of a specific philosophical lan-

guage). The nature of this right cannot be considered indepen-
dently from its curious duplicity. It is indeed, as we shall see, a right
of absolute property, according to the Roman formula of such a
right: *jus utendi et abutendi*—it is a right of excess. But it is also, simultaneously, the right of approximation—the almost of a *right*
[*l'à-peu-près d'un* droit].

In the *Science of Logic*, introducing the section on "objectivity,"
Hegel writes: "Philosophy has the right to select from the language of common life which is made for the world of pictorial
thinking, such expressions as *seem to approximate* [scheinen . . .
nahe kommen] to the determinations of the concept" (*SL*, 708).
The good fortune to find a speculative word seems therefore to be
turned into a decision that pertains only to certain appearances,
effects, or reflects [*Schein*] of language. And in fact, the gap between the posited concept and the excluded meanings, which, in
the Remark on the *aufheben*, has continually amazed us, is now
somewhat justified (in thought the lexical stage would be used
only for certain of its effects and not for itself; "the word, the speculative," can also be stated in this way: "a word [seems to approx-
imate] the speculative"). But this however entails that the text,
which we are now reading, should formally contradict everything
that the text on the Remark, at least through its movement, led us
to expect. For Hegel continues: "There cannot be any question of
demonstrating [erweisen] for a word selected from the language of
common life that in common life, too, one associates [*verbinden*]
with it the same concept for which philosophy employs it [*gebrauchen*]; for common life has no concept, but only pictorial
thoughts and general ideas, and to recognize the concept in what
is else a mere general idea is philosophy itself" (*SL*, 708).

On the one hand, the concept is therefore not in language but
in philosophy (a sharper distinction—in fact, a distinction of another nature—than the one that elsewhere distinguishes "naïve"

language and learned speculation), and, the passage from representation to philosophical thought, on the other hand, seems to be the passage from a tie—from a *Verbindung*—between word and concept (a semiological regime) to a recognition (without further precision) of the concept *of* word, or at least of *that*, of a neuter that would appear to hesitate between the word and representation.—Now it is indeed a hesitation that is at issue, a floating, of which one must make the most for thinking. The text indeed adds:

> It must suffice [*genügen*] therefore if pictorial thinking, [*bei*] in the use of its expressions that are employed for philosophical determinations, has before it some vague idea [*vorschwebt—sich vorschweben*—is "to have a vague idea"—and *jemandem etwas vorschweben*, is "to delude somebody into believing," "to pull somebody's leg"] of their distinctive meaning [*von ihrem Unterschiede*];[13] just as it may be the case that in these [*bei jenen*: probably those which were at issue two sentences before] expressions one recognizes nuances [*Schattierungen*] of pictorial thought that are more closely related [*näher*] to the corresponding concepts. (*SL*,708)

And a little further, having evoked the example of the word *to be* and *to exist* [*existieren*, a word without purism . . .], Hegel concludes that if, in communal life, they can be synonymous (in other words, if their synonymy brings about a play of *Schattierung*), "philosophy will in any case be free to utilize such empty superfluity of language for its distinctions" (*SL*, 709).

The right of philosophy is thus not exactly a right of property. It might rather be something like the right of salvage.[14] Philosophy is free to seize what remains superfluous in language. It is the use and the accommodation of remnants. A remnant is here, for example, a synonymy, the useless surplus of a word—and hence, an *empty* word. The finds that, in language, are ready for the delight of the speculative thinker do not belong to the strict economy of language, are not a matter of the "needs" of the lexicon and of grammar; they are rather what escapes from such an economy—a superfluity for the purpose of the exactness of representation, a generosity toward speculation. The empty word, on whose relief the dialectical process is organized, is not so much emptied out by the philosophical analysis of "being" (strictly speaking, there is no such analysis at the beginning of the *Science of Logic*) as it is found, empty, in language or in an emptiness of language. It looks as though the "speculative spirit" of language consisted in comprehending, in language, the being-for-speculation as the word *being*, an empty and superfluous synonym—or in constituting the speculative process as the surplus over its twofold meaning that the word *aufheben* entails. In this emptiness—or in this overabundance—words float; they are approximate—they come, without reaching them, near concepts, which, as we read, "correspond," without it being possible to know exactly what they correspond to (to the words? to the representations?) nor exactly what such a correspondence might be. The *näher* of precision—as the one that, in a "more particular determination" of the *aufheben*, calls for the word *Moment*—is in fact also the *näher* of approximation, of the nearly [*de l'à peu-près*]. It is on this paradoxical mode that one deals with the term (gets nearer to the term) that clarifies the *aufheben* in its reflexivity. And it is indeed, let us recall, as a "fitting" [*passend*] determination that *Moment* was introduced. In its word the precise effectiveness of the dialectical lever functions like a wavering, which makes—the reader, perhaps—in any case, the text *work*.[15] Speculative thought meets with its fortune and its delight in the realm of nuances—*Schattierung*: the realm of the chiaroscuro, of the plays of shadow in a misty light.—The staging of the lexicon is therefore not challenged under the heading of theatrical illusion; it is rather too simple and too clear a stage. The speculative stage is a shadow theater—curiously like another cave, a cave that, this time, would seem to be dug in full day light, right next to the sun [*à même le soleil*].

In the play of shadows one only distinguishes the reliefs of the contour—(one only distinguishes the *an*, the indistinct passage of form to its own edge)—but this is precisely how figures are formed, as the text of the *Aesthetics* shows, to which we must go back.

In the *Aesthetics* the semiological convention is recalled for introducing us to the symbol (hence, the order adopted in the Remarks of the *Science of Logic*, which goes from the symbol to language, and which followed in the theory of language in the *Encyclopedia*, is, up to a point, reversed—even though in *Phantasie* the symbol, the allegory, and the *Dichtung* go together). The symbol is above all determined by its ambiguity [*Zweifelhaftigkeit*],[16] which consists in the joint presentation of a meaning and a sensory existence.[17] It is in the regime of this essential ambiguity that the "conscious symbolic" develops the art of figures, rhetoric in general in the third chapter. But it is in the course of the same development that, unexpectedly, the status of speculative words, or of the language of the concept, will be clarified.

In the introduction the specificity of the symbol is already underlined through the examination of the following question: "whether such a picture [for example, the lion], as we say, *is to be taken literally or at the same time metaphorically*, or even perhaps [*oder auch etwa*] *only metaphorically* [nur uneigentlich]" (*A*, 1:306). The first case is not examined: it is of course that of the sign, and everyone knows what its "property" is worth. The second case is the symbolic one. The third—the one that comes with a precaution: *etwa* (perhaps, if by any chance, almost, approximately, in some ways)—an almost improbable case, is the one Hegel first illustrates:

The latter is the case, e.g., with symbolical expressions in speech, with words like *begreifen*, *schliessen*, and so forth. When these signify spiritual activities [i.e. comprehending or concluding], we have immediately before our minds only their meaning of a spiritual activity without recalling [*erinnern*] at all [*etwa*] at the same time the visible actions of touching [*begreifen*] or closing [*schliessen*]. But in the picture of a lion there confronts us not only the meaning which it may have as a symbol, but also this visible shape and existent. (*A*, 1:306)

Next to the symbol, then, kept away from it, the language of the concept is posited and posits its major concepts: the concept, the syllogism, as determined acceptations (determined *meaning* [sens]). It is, as it were, in flagrant contradiction with the speculative law of the *aufheben* of meaning [*sens*]—unless the "meaning" of the *aufheben* should precisely pass through it.

Indeed, it passes through it; that is to say that it goes through this special category (this quasi, not to say this pseudo-, category) of the "symbolic expression," which is neither symbol (sensory presence) nor sign (conventional meaning). The word, the speculative, passes between these two meanings—such as, for example, in addition to *begreifen* or *schliessen*, the dazzling word *meaning* [sens], which was attracting our attention in the *Aesthetics* a few chapters ago: "'Sense' is this wonderful [*wunderbar*] word which is used in two opposite meanings. On the one hand it means the organ of immediate apprehension [*Auffassung*], but on the other hand we mean by it the sense, the significance, the thought, the universal underlying the thing [*Sache*]" (*A*, 1:128). (This word, this speculative meaning, is then invoked in the first moment of the beautiful, natural beauty, the first sublation of the matter and the concept of aesthetics—the primary meaning of the whole of philosophical aesthetics.)—Such a passage between meaning and meaning [*sens et sens*], the remainder or the relief of meaning and of "meaning" [*de sens et du "sens"*] is clarified in the conscious symbolism of the metaphor, where, once again, the language of the concept returns: "In the first place, every language already contains a mass of metaphors. They arise from the fact that a word which originally signifies only something sensuous is carried over [*übertragen*] into the spiritual sphere. *Fassen, begreifen*, and many words, to speak generally, which relate to knowing."[18] These spontaneous metaphors of language, however, "gradually . . . vanish [disappear]" and "if, for example, we are to take *begreifen* in a spiritual sense, then it does not occur to us at all to think of a perceptible grasping by the hand" (ibid.).

The philosophical word is thus a vanished metaphor—it was already the vanishing of a literal meaning [*sens propre*]. From the outset the determined, literal meaning has been reduced by the convention without origin of language. The metaphor, here, would appear to stand for a place of origin—of an origin admittedly still itself without origin,[19] but at least, it might be the only drifting movement along which meaning, the remainder of meaning, which leads to "spiritual meaning," that is, to "speculative meaning," can be apprehended.—Now, from whence does this metaphor come? Or else, as Hegel says, what is "the sense and aim of metaphorical diction [*Diktion*] in general"?[20] This meaning and this aim consist in "join[ing] two things together into one [*fügen*—to adjoin, to fold, to subject—the double *(Zweifach)* in(to) the one *(Eins)*]" (ibid.): it is thus a meaning and a goal of the *aufheben*, or, at least, it is not surprising to find the sublation of the twofold meaning at the end—if it is an end—of the slow vanishing of metaphor (one always finds the speculative calculation again through the operation of the vanishing magnitude, the conceptual calculation through the metaphorical derivative, and the textual calculation through differential *Schattierung . . .*).—But the "meaning" of metaphor, of "metaphorical diction" itself, has multiple grounds [*une raison multiple*], which Hegel enumerates in this way:

(a) first, the "reinforcement" of the feelings or of the passions that the poet expresses—a reinforcement insofar as the self (of the hero, of the poet) expresses its "grip on all sorts of ideas" (*A*, 1:406);

(b) then, and as if at a higher level than the first one, the will of the spirit, which, although it plunges into the objects, "it still

wishes to free itself from their externality, because in the external it seeks *itself* and spiritualizes it; and now by shaping itself and its passion into something beautiful, it evinces its
power to bring into representation [*Darstellung*] its elevation
[*Erhebung*] above everything external" (*A*, 1:407).

Admittedly, *Erhebung* is not *Aufhebung*—and, as far as the positive meaning of the latter is concerned, it is a matter of a
Schattierung. But the *Darstellung* is the matter of the *aufheben*, and
the *aufheben* is indeed the process through which the speculative itself is found and presented on the outside, in the word. The *Grund*
of metaphor has a rigorous structure of *aufheben*. A little later, let
us add, while ending the chapter on metaphor, Hegel indicates
that Schiller has a style that, even in prose, is rich in metaphors and
in figures in general, since he makes an "effort to express deep concepts as to bring them before our minds without pressing on to the
strictly philosophical expression of thought. In his work, then, the
inherently rational and speculative unity sees and finds its counterpart in the life of the present world" (*A*, 1:408). Metaphor is thus not
philosophical language; it is even in fact the reverse or the opposite
image of it: *Gegen-bild*; but it is separated from it—as from its
"own" vanishing—only by the fleeting glare of a mirror, perhaps
once again by a *Schattierung*. In any case the speculative is *seen* and
is *found* (happy surprise) as a figure in the figure. That is to say that
speculation incidentally has itself, in Hegel's text, been meta-
phorized ("speculative unity sees . . . its counterpart"). In many
ways (which remain plural, which do not form a system, which go
through what might be a doctrine of the literal meaning and a doctrine of the primitive figure), then, the figure, which is vanishing,
spiritualized but exterior, reflected, takes an active, albeit *discreet*,
part in the presentation of the speculative in the Hegelian text.

This text is also, after all, that of the *Phenomenology of Spirit*,
which ends, without interrupting its syntax, with two of Schiller's

verses, which form its ultimate figure, the sublating reading of which ought to know precisely how to present Absolute Knowledge, its last word, right at the level of its form:

the two together, comprehended History, form alike the inwardizing and the Calvary of absolute Spirit, the actuality, truth and certainty of his throne, without which he would be lifeless and alone. Only

> *aus dem Kelche dieses Geisterreiches*
> *schaümt ihm seine Unendlichkeit.*[21]

Hegel does not indicate the origin of these verses; the figure is not quoted—it is recited by rote.

Can its relief (remnant) be sublated?

No doubt, the metaphorical approach or approximation is always—in conformity with the whole of the philosophical and rhetorical tradition concerning the figure in general—waiting to be identified. Figure: one expects that the mask will fall, and that the "foam" of infinity will be dissipated in front of the genuine face of spirit, which it really merely promises. But we should no doubt have said enough here for suspecting that this wait, this expectation and this promise, might be indefinitely prolonged. Not because of a regrettable infirmity of our means of expression (as the same tradition has always decreed it): since, as we know, it is indeed right at the level of language that speculative thought sublates and presents (itself) [*(se) relève et (se) présente*]. Speculative language is not figurative language; but it *is* not, it *is* especially not, what this simple negative *proposition* could lead us to believe. Along the vanishings or the driftings of figures, strokes of luck occur—approximately. And, if you like, this can approximately and figuratively be called "speculative language."[22] Speculative language is founded upon and contents itself with (*es genügt*) approximation. Between *its* approximation and that of metaphor, between two shadows on this stage, Hegel does not allow us to decide, and his text in fact carefully, discreetly, and subtly fosters indecision. Something of the figure remains in relief (as a remnant).

Hence, in the Remark it was impossible to decide on the status of *Moment*: is it a mechanical metaphor? Assuredly, but in order to determine such an important concept as that of the *aufheben*, Hegel then speaks like Schiller, and the lever is but a reflection; is it, on the contrary, a "true" mechanics? But we know that no mechanism is truly true, just as none of language's words are truly "literal" [*propre*] (and that in the mechanical memory both yet constitute the empty form right at the level of which rational content is thought). There remains, for the *Moment*, nothing but Hegel's "own" expression: a meaning "*only* metaphorical" (*A*, 1:306), an expression that cannot not have rather been taken from the metaphorical register, an expression picked up from the figure's relief [*prelevée sur le relief de la figure*]. If *to read* (or to exhibit), and to read the *aufheben* is to sublate language and the propositions that we read, *aufheben* might be only to know how to hear this metaphorical remainder.

The Word: Relief

There thus remains a word, and more precisely, that is, more confusedly or more approximately, there remain Hegel's words—just as there remains, as if to prove the extent to which reading is constrained by one of Hegel's redoubtable laws, a word: *relief*—a floating relief, an artificial and deceitful island, the remainder and the cunning of sublation.

Why do Hegelian words, Hegelian bons mots remain? Why does the Remark on the *aufheben* resist to such an extent (that is, to such a small extent—but always only ever so small) every effort to reduce it, to explain it, to follow its *meaning* in the system. Why should the circle of circles, instead of annulling the auxiliary remark of a word, multiply and scatter, from circle to circle, its distorting effects?

> (*But just as well: why does the system resist every effort to be reduced to the core of the aufheben, to be condensed at this point? The aufheben—at least as far as its Remark is concerned [but where else to find its concept?]—is not the speculum of the system, it rather diffracts it, it breaks or makes its rays deviate, it blurs the East and the West.*)

There remain words because one must speak, because philosophy must speak—and neither for ensuring Professor Hegel's retributions or the social power of his discourse—at least, not only or simply. One must speak because the disappearance of words, of speculative words (all that remains of words when thought is sublated), might hand us over to the most redoubtable threat—a threat that is hidden somewhere in philosophy itself, in reason, and that, for this very reason, thought must crucially *sublate*.

This threat is twofold, or rather it presents itself as a double figure. It is not a coincidence if we will not be able to interrogate this duplicity for itself right to the last—that is, to reduce it. But let us first of all uncover this twofold figure [*ce double visage*].

The first one is that of madness—(and we know, let us note straight away, that this face has always been at once hideous, troubling, terrible, and comic).

In the midst of the process of sublation of the name in memory and in thought—in the midst, then, of the process of the loss of meaning of words—Hegel has broken off (it is the Addition to § 462 of the *Encyclopedia*) in order to give the word, as if for the first and last time, its most pronounced relief: "The true, concrete negativity of the language-sign is *intelligence*, since by this the sign is changed from something outward to something inward and as thus transformed is preserved. . . . The articulated sound, the *word*, is alone such an inward externality" (*Enc. III*, § 462:221). The word itself is thus and is only the product of the *aufheben*, whose moments are here clearly articulated. And the *aufheben* of the word, or the *aufgehoben* that the word is, merges with a form— *umgestaltet*, that is, "transformed," but also, "reversed," and "deformed." But what is to deform a form? What is this new expression that has just slipped at the point of the *aufheben* (where the word should be the sublation of a material form and of an ideal content) and that cannot, any more than the syntactical *an*, be reduced, grasped—*begreifen*—since in fact, it itself remains the condition of the *begreifen* and, moreover, the status of the word *Begriff*, among many others? What is this yet so decisive *aufheben*, where the sign is not sublated in the element of thought but transformed or deformed into a word. It *is* nothing—nothing but this *Schattierung* between two names of the form, *Gestalt* and *Form*, a play of shadow where the passage, the transformation or the deformation of form, occurs right at the level of form—nothing but this sliding and this subtle torsion of language that allows us to constrain, to bend over and to adjoin (*fügen* is, as we saw, the "meaning" of the metaphor) words to an *Ausdruck*, to a turn, to an effect, to a *façon de dire*. Nothing but a subtly twisted form.

This twisted form, however, protects us from the greatest danger. "To want to think without words as Mesmer once attempted is, therefore, a manifestly irrational procedure [*Unvernunft*] which, as Mesmer himself admitted, almost drove him insane [*Wahnsinn*]" (*Enc. III*, § 462:221). *This man*, Hegel writes (or Michelet, it is an addition), thus underlining the stakes, which are not that of the thesis or of the experience of an author but that of humanity, here and there, and for example, here where Hegel, the man, speaks and writes.[23] Between Hegel and madness, between (speculative) reason and the unsettling of reason, lies the thin barrier—relief—of a strange, twisted form, whose twisting forms—or deforms—the *aufheben*. Even then, this protection might not be as secure as one might wish it to be. For Hegel refuses to give words an auxiliary status, that of mercenaries or nurses of reason. Thought is actualized in words—and therefore, if the threat of madness is averted (which also means that it has come very close [*est passée tout près*] and that thought has felt its disquieting proximity), then, at the same time, another disquieting figure emerges, precisely insofar as thought refuses or avoids to be handed over to the "inexpressible" or to the "ineffable."[24] We already know this figure, but it is blurred and it becomes stranger in this text: it is the mad figure of mechanical thought, of thought *actually* mechanical:

> Intelligence, therefore, in filling itself [*erfüllt*: to fill up with] with the word, receives into itself [*aufnimmt*: it gathers up; it is the word that one uses for "taking the gauntlet" or for "recording"] the nature of the thing. But this reception [*Aufnahme*] has, at the same time, the meaning that intelligence thereby takes on the nature of a *thing* [*sich zu einem Sächlichen macht*] and to such a degree that subjectivity, in its distinction from the thing, becomes quite empty, a mindless container of words, that is, a mechanical memory. In this way the *profusion* [*Übermaß*] of *remembered words* [Erinnerung] can, so to speak, switch round [*umschlägt*] to become the extreme *alienation* of intelligence. The more familiar I become with the meaning of the word, the more, therefore, that this becomes united with my inwardness, the more can the objectivity, and hence the definiteness, of meaning, vanish and consequently the more can memory itself, and with it also the words, become something bereft of mind [*zu etwas Geistesverlassenem werden*].[25]

The mechanical is in general the place of a dialectical exteriority because the latter is always on the point of exceeding and of blocking speculation. One here reads—and for once, one reads Hegel's "own" enunciation, Hegel who says "I": one thus also hears—that there is, in fact, at the heart of the process of thought, an overloading, a surplus under whose weight intelligence founders. In this foundering, spirit disappears—at the surface of the abyss, there remain only words, these pieces of wreckage. (Notably, the wreckage of a lever. The *Moment* itself falls over from the ideal to the real from the "line" to the "weight"—or: the weight of interiority is excessive, and the lever remains blocked. Is this weight—*Gewicht*—not the weight of the concept—"*einer der* wichtigsten *Begriffe*"? What is thrown overboard during the wreckage might well be the heavy concept of *aufheben*.)

Admittedly, this foundering will have taken place so as to do more and better than to prevent or to cure madness; it will have taken place in order purely and simply to annul even its possibility, its threat, however remote it may be (but we know that it is quite close . . .). But to annul it is both to give oneself the chance to suppress it and to run the risk of preserving it: an *aufheben* in itself broken is at work in this text,[26] which, instead of sublating together thought and its other, leaves two figures face to face: that of an averted dementia—and opposite (for, as we could indeed learn, conjuration might precisely take part in dementia), a thought that scuppers itself [*qui se saborde*]. It will always be possible and necessary to say that *for Hegel* this scuppering is decided, organized, guaranteed—and perhaps also only mimed. But it will be impossible to ignore the fact that from that point on, *Hegel's text* is nonetheless doomed never to finding or to finding its meaning (its direction) again, since it is meaning that has been thrown overboard and since this loss will always be carefully preserved, instead of being made good, at the decisive moments of speculation, and first of all, at the remarkable "moment" of the *aufheben*. (One is therefore rather led to believe the following: having organized the speculative staging of the wreckage, and determined to present it in the most realist manner through its discourse and its words, Hegel suddenly would appear to have lost control of the staging, a "real" wreckage might have taken place. Yet as the tradition in the world of theater would have it, the show must go on. It must go on even if we know that it is only a game *and* that a redoubtable, mortal *actuality* is at play in this game. Such might be the almost unbearable experience of Hegelian discourse (bearable, however, and sublatable because taking place as discourse [*discourue*]). The disappearance of meaning might resemble Molière's death. Let us note that, in spite of everything, the mechanism nowhere can be sublated—or be sublated "entirely," if one dare say so—as we have no doubt sufficiently demonstrated here.—And because there is no "inexpressible," one should even note that, in Hegel's text, between these pages that continually flutter and founder in turn, the knowledge of this loss without return (without *aufheben* or, more precisely, in the *middle* of the *aufheben* "itself") circulates. It does so very strangely, through the dislocated, halting, and desperate form of these texts, which attempt to constitute the impossible discourse outside meaning [*hors du sens*] (after the wreckage, for speaking in water). But this knowledge is an obscure, singular, perhaps mechanical knowledge, lost at the bottom of the sea, buried under the dispersed wreckages. What is at issue is not madness but the disquieting figure that a very ancient sculpted figure at the bow of philosophy might have here taken [*figure sculptée à la proue de la philosophie*]: Socrates, or knowledge that knows how not to know, having become, in a twisted form, the word that "knows" itself no longer to mean anything— but what does a word that is no longer intelligible "know"? . . . Socrates having become stupid, dazed, "mechanical" [*méchanique*], as one used to say in Old French.

It is nevertheless a fact that Hegel's discourse is also devoted to restoring, to elevating [*relever*] the figure of Socrates[27] and that the exposition of this discourse does not, in spite of everything, sink into madness. On the contrary. In any case, it matters if it does not sink into the kind of madness that can be diagnosed—whatever the case may be around discourses of diagnostic and the "knowledge" that authorizes them. There is no question of affirming that Hegel is mad: the readiness of the paradox would immediately undermine it. It has only been a question of discerning, in the shadow of a threat that is never directly confronted, the subtle twist, the minute but irretrievable gesture, to which discourse is constrained; because it neither wants nor risks madness, it refuses to relinquish its mastery and its "*property.*" On the contrary, it hopes to master the presentation of the speculative absolute *and* posits this presentation right at the level of the empty form of words and of propositions that the spirit has deserted: a twofold gesture that bears only one "name," *aufheben.*—It is for this reason that another figure, which insinuates itself even more discreetly, remains to be identified in the place of or beside what we called, only in passing, "madness."

The twisting of form indeed always risks to take another turn, which Hegel painstakingly avoids. It is the turn of the *Witz*—that is, of the witticism [*trait d'esprit*]—or of the spirit *tout court*, of this *Gegenbild* of the *Geist* that threatens to occupy the space the latter abandons—that is to say, still of another "bon mot" that might be threatening the empty word, the speculative.[28]

What is at issue is still, to begin, the relief of the figure or, more precisely, of what remains to be read concerning metaphor. We did not exhaust a few pages ago its multiple "reasons." There remained the following third *Grund*:

But even so, *thirdly*, the metaphorical expression may arise from the purely bacchanalian delight of fancy [*die schwelgerische Lust*—as we know, we must simultaneously translate: of the purely luxurious pleasure] . . . or . . . from the wit [*Witz*] of a subjective caprice [*Willkür*] which, to escape from the commonplace, surrenders to a piquant [*pikant*] impulse, not satisfied until it has succeeded in finding related traits in the apparently most heterogeneous [*heterogenste*] material and therefore, to our astonishment, combining things [*kombinieren*] that are poles apart from one another. (*A*, 1:407)

There is thus this other possible "reason" of metaphor, which, as we see, juts out. It is kept apart from the other two insofar as the whole of this sentence is pejorative—and insofar as it can here save us the trouble of going through Hegel's other texts in order to establish the debasing or the rejection of the *Witz*. With respect to the other metaphorical functions, it pushes aside a nonserious genre, which is not serious for two reasons, the one more "moral," the other more "logical," but which, from the speculative thinker's point of view, form a single combination. On the one hand, the *Witz* is at best a matter of luxury, at the worst of debauchery and, in any case, of a shallow pleasure; on the other hand, it is a matter of an unbridled excitation, handed over to the disorder of heterogeneousness and to the chimeras of "combinations."—If metaphor, among its other functions, had a structure of *aufheben*, and if figures, while vanishing, had to give rise to the literality of speculative concepts, it goes without saying that the *Witz* cannot fulfill this role or correspond to this structure. The *Witz* must be avoided.

But to the extent that we do not know—at least not clearly and not conceptually—what allows us to distinguish rigorously, between these two metaphorical products, the one that comes from the *Geist* in search of its self, and the one that risks coming from the disorders of the *Witz*—and to the more precise extent that the criterion of such a distinction is in any case found outside the word (seemingly in a moral and/or logical and/or aesthetic judgment), it is highly probable that one might here be faced with one of the reasons, and not the least important one of them, of what will have prevented the actual dialectical articulation of the speculative to the metaphorical word. The domain of metaphor, with its three possible "reasons," is too confused: one might always risk to take a *Witz* for a concept. (And, does the *Witz* as a combination of elements so remote that they might be opposed, not strangely resemble an *aufheben*? Are we not seeing it, moreover, keep company with *Phantasie*, which is sublating and which produces both fictions and words? It is the resemblance that creates the danger of confusion: it is no doubt not a coincidence if this situation recalls the danger of confusion between the sophist and the philosopher to which one comes very close in Plato's *Sophist*—that is, the *Witz*

*soph*ist/philo*soph*er with which the philosopher must indeed cross
swords and get caught. In order to avoid the *Witz*, metaphor and
more generally the whole order of figuration should be altogether
avoided. That is to say that, under the heading of concept one will
expressly avoid retaining anything of this order, the enumeration
of which, in the "Riddle," begins by pointing to the first species of
"the conscious wit [*Witz*] of symbolism" (*A*, 1:398), and thus with
a formation that, in spite of a rich history, "has sunk down more
or less to conversation and mere witticisms and jokes [*Spaß*] in social gatherings" (ibid.)[29]—and which moreover continues by pointing to the play on words, which is its most trivial form: "To the riddle we may append that infinitely wide field of witty [*witzige*] and
striking notions [*frappierende Einfälle*], which are developed as
plays on words [*Wortspiel*], and epigrams [*Sinngedicht*] . . ." (ibid.).

The play on words, the word that plays—this is eventually all
that remains of the word caught in the *Witz* and threatened by the
figure; it is its last relief (remainder) or its scrap. And this condemnation, or at least this warning—which is addressed to
buffoonery, if not to madness—is curiously closely akin to the
speculative refusal of verbal speculation. That one be playing or
thinking on the basis of *a word* is no doubt the same thing, the
same "Frivolität" of which Hegel elsewhere taxes the *Witz*.[30] As
Kombination, a turn of phrase [*tour d'un mot*] or a pleasant combination of words, speculation can only be a mystification. This
is what Hegel reproaches as violently to Jacobi as to Hamann, as
we read as an epigraph to this work. Hamann, in particular, is the
one who, against the *Aufklärung* and against Kant, has continually raised the problem of the *coincidentia oppositorum*,[31] that is to
say, the very problem or matter of the *aufheben*. But Hamann answers only by means of jokes, or *plaisanteries*, by means of *mots*
[*Witz*]. (Hegel thus does not even discuss the Hamannian theo-
ries of language and of the *Witz*. He offers only this objection:
"Hamann . . . did not take the trouble which, if one dare say so,

God has taken, of developing the concentrated nucleus of truth
. . . into a system.")[32]

A *bon mot* cannot resolve the *coincidentia oppositorum*; *aufheben*
cannot be a *Witz*. And it is indeed what the Remark on the
aufheben discreetly states in the last sentence that we still have to
reread: "The double-meaning of the Latin *tollere* (which has become famous through the Ciceronian pun *tollendum est Octavium*)
does not go so far" (*SL*, 107). Attention is drawn to the word, the
Latin word, closest to *aufheben* by means of a *Witz*. And Hegel, in
turn, avoids this word: for, according to the lexicon, the two meanings of *tollere* form a structure very close to that of the *aufheben*.
And in order to avoid *tollere*, Hegel is obliged to have recourse to
a semantic nuance in a somewhat deceitful manner (for his remark
does not touch on the simultaneous presence of two opposite
meanings): "its affirmative determination signifies only a lifting-up
[*Emporheben*]." A *Schattierung* of meaning, between *Emporheben*
and *Aufheben* in the positive sense, barely ensures the privilege of
the German word. What have we gained? We have gained not to
fall in the common property of many languages; we have protected ourselves from an excessive dispersion. It will indeed suffice,
a little later, to grant Latin with some reflexive necessity. But at the
same time, we have averted any confusion with the *Witz*. The first
of these speculative words has nothing to do with a *bon mot*.

It is no doubt what one must read here. Hegel does not yet state
this thesis as such. The *Witz* is brushed aside underhandedly so
that the thesis as such almost vanishes. The brushing aside is only,
according to the text, the bracketing of an anecdotal indication (of
a *bon mot* reported by Cicero). The *Witz*, whose concept is absolutely not examined, is but a word that finds itself here by
chance. It is a coincidence—the *coincidentia* of the opposite that
the *Witz* and the *aufheben* are—and this coincidence is not resolved. In the discourse of the Remark there is thus an ultimate remainder (relief): the word *Witz*.—That is to say that there is, in all

of Hegel's texts, those remainders of the *Witz* that are *also* as many *bons* mots (as many *right* words) and that are even plays on words: "*Dinge-Denken.*" This mechanical alarm is just as much a joke as the combination of the most heterogeneous things. As if, not having expressly or rigorously been excluded, the *Witz*, too, "repeatedly occurred"—unless its exclusion be subtly kept (almost) silent in order to allow it to return. . . .

Hegel does not tell—and this refusal is the last guarantee against what his discourse refuses without respite, against verbal speculation. This refusal means—or at least indicates—the refusal to count on any word and to count on *the speculation of the (absolute) signified in a signifier*, such as, up until Hegel, the whole of philosophy has in various ways speculated on it, that is to say, played out and counted both its losses and its benefits, the benefits and the bankruptcies of a meaning [*sens*] and a truth, which Hegel has definitely carried along in the entirely other and ambiguous operation of the *aufheben* (unless one should prefer to say that, in this speculation, the Hegelian *aufheben* gambles for the first time the *whole* stake or *all* the capital of meaning [*toute la mise ou tout le capital du sens*]).

But this refusal henceforth also carries along what constrains words to be written irresolutely in Hegelian discourse, from text to text, between *Aufheben* and *Witz*. Verbal speculation can be averted only by avoiding to *sublate* these words. The very operation of the *aufheben* entails, in all its rigor and in all its necessity, a remainder, the relief of its own—forever improper—nonsublated *Witz*. A *Witz*, or some nonsublated *Witz*, this might not be unrelated to this restlessness, this agitation—*Unruhe*—where we *almost* saw Hegel write the expression of the speculative, as if *right at the level* [à même] of the defects of propositional discourse. The *Witz* "is" blurred; it blurs grammar, logic—it troubles Hegel himself, as we read. Hegel's "painful effort," the desperate effort of the speculative, might be an effort *not* to master this unrest, *even* while identifying and sublating it. . . .

6

Epilogue

A book is a thing and each of its leaves is also a thing, and so too is each bit of its pages, and so on to infinity.

—Hegel, *Hegel's Science of Logic*

(*Epilogue: two things are at issue. First of all, a certain turn of mind [esprit], the* "es-prit d'épilogue" *[spirit of epilogue] which is the* "*disposition to epilogize, to find fault with something.*" *Hegel would find fault with what we are saying. Then an epilogue, something which is only appended to discourse, in fact like a Remark, which extends it, but which also escapes it, which might cover it, but which in any case exceeds it.*)

Yet the *Witz* is sublated. But what does *yet* mean here? Nothing but "consequently." The *Witz* is thus sublated—it is so from the outset; it has always been so, since the whole of language, all its possible mechanisms, all the play on its meanings have always been submitted to the *unheard-of* constraint of the *aufheben*, which cannot but have "returned" to the *Witz* too. Better, it might first be to the *Witz* that the *aufheben* returns: the coincidence of the Remark must also, of course, above all be read as the sublation of Latin by German and of the *Witz* by the *Aufheben*. The general law of the system does not tolerate an exception. The one who thinks that he has *resolved* Hegel's discourse by proclaiming that its major concept is a word, a "word," a *bon mot*, would cut a sorry figure. For should he believe that he has thus revealed the secret of the absolute, the absolute might tell him that it has always been laid bare, right at the level of words, that when all is said and done its secret is an open secret. Should one, on the contrary, imagine being able to make Hegel a laughingstock, to hold him to ridicule, he would still be offering empty words, for since the latter suppress all determinate meaning, they all the more forbid us play on meanings [*jouer sur les sens*].

Consequently, if one thought of being able to inscribe, under the heading of the *Witz*, an ultimate relief, it cannot have been by following either of these gestures but rather by submitting to the demand of a repetition of the very operation that leaves or produces this relief (remnant). It is also in this way that Hegel must now feel compelled to revise.—That the *Witz* be *and* not be sublated (to speak by propositions . . .) in fact necessarily entails that there is no Hegelian *bon mot* in *any sense* of the word. It is the logic of the *aufheben*—but, as we already know, to begin with, this logic also brings about this irresistible passage or this unavoidable passage from one word to the other, to begin, from *aufheben* to *Moment*. A plural, difficult, dispersed, aleatory usage is substituted for the accuracy and for the excellence of the words learnedly chosen—and even more for the precision of the constructed *terms*—between play and seriousness. This "usage" (another name or another side of what we called a "calculation") cannot be understood as a lack, an insufficiency of this logic, but rather as its innermost turn:

its cycle—*Kreislauf*—and its *façon de parler*—*Ausdruck*. The logical turn, as it is set out in the *Science of Logic*, consists of the permanent, continual—yet discreet and discontinuous—unsettling, through all its text, of any function of "bon mot." The *Science of Logic* consists of disconcerting its own book by scattering remarkable words in it. Such dispersion will always prevent the syntax or the composition of the book from reducing them to any identity of meaning. If there is or if there remains something that can be called a "Witz" of the *Science of Logic*, it is assuredly not an identity or a truth, whether or not it be obtained playfully, but it might be nothing else but this economy of use [*économie d'usage*], the heterogeneous combination that *also* forms its "logic." And it is such an unsettling, its sliding, its mechanism, its broken means, that is called the "text," to use a more or less empty word too.[1]

Such a disruption occurs in the *Science of Logic* just as much from the outside as from the inside of its system. From the outside, if, as we tried to show, Hegel has already gambled all the available assets. For it goes without saying [*il va "de soi"*] that the unavoidable disruptiveness of a repetition of the *aufheben after* Hegel and a few others is alone likely to escape a speculation in which, quite simply, it is henceforth difficult to see what or how to invest. But also from the inside, since, as we noted throughout our reading, it is the law of the system as it lets itself be read, be given over to this subtle and discreet disorder. It is the law of the system, in particular, that allows us to pass from a Remark, from the logic of being to that of determinate being. That is to say that this passage occurs through the relief (the witticism) [*saillie*] of a word—*aufheben*—and a word that the Remark, in conclusion, already carries along outside itself, toward other words, other determinations, first of all toward *Dasein*, the empirical, hazardous, accidental existence of things and words. Let us recall this text, the epilogue of the Remark: "The more precise meaning and expression which being and nothing receive, now that they are *moments*, is to be ascertained from the consideration of determinate being as the unity in which they are preserved" (*SL*, 107–8).

The *aufheben* is engaged in approximation on its own accord [*de soi*]; it gives itself over to the chance and the accidents of the plural of words, to the comma that one must indeed write between the word and the speculative. The word will not come out unscathed. It will end up, if not by being dissolved, at least by brushing against dissolution. Dissolution—the *Auflösung*—is the word that precedes the *aufheben* in the *Logic*, before, if you will, the beginning of the *Aufheben*. It is also the word that, in Hegel's texts, will increasingly brush against or even blur with its shadow—*Schattierung*—the word *aufheben*.

Auflösen is first of all the substitute of the *aufheben* in the physicochemical process, that is, in the process or the moment of the neutral (that is to say, [the moment of] water), at the heart of the *Philosophy of Nature*, at the "core" of the system (and, above all, at the heart of "objectivity," itself at the "core" of the logic of the concept). The *Auflösung* no doubt arises preferably at the time of negative separation (cf., for example, *Enc. II*, § 287). The latter, dissociation or dislocation, the simple negative of an *aufheben*, is, however, called separation [*Diremtion*, § 324], sundering [*Zerfallen*, § 291, and *Zerlegen*, § 308], decomposition [*Zersetzen*, § 330], and so forth. The *Auflösung* itself rather indicates a dissolution like the one that heat operates and following which "in realizing itself or as actually realized, this consumption of bodily peculiarity comes to exist as pure physical ideality" (§ 306:171), in "the moment of real *dissolution* of the *immediacy* of specified material things" (§ 307:157), before being the double movement of exchange and mixture of the neutral (§ 333): "The dissociation of the neutral body is the beginning of its reversion to particular chemical bodies, back to their indifference through a series of processes which are, on the one hand, peculiar; each such dissociation [*Scheidung*] is, on the other hand, itself inseparably linked with a combination [*Vereinigung*]."[2]

The displacement of the structure of the *aufheben* into an
auflösen in chemistry might explain what, in this process, cannot
yet be sublation and that must be sublated: for sublation belongs
to the *life* of the teleological process, just as, in the *Science of Logic*,
it belongs to the life of the concept. The *auflösen* before the
aufheben, the anteriority of the *Logic* repeated in the *Philosophy of
Nature*, might oblige us to conceive a delay of the *aufheben* on itself [*un retard de l'aufheben sur lui-même*], a sort of dissolution of
its process in its own beginning, just as in its neutral moment. The
water in which the voice of the *aufheben* speaks might be dissolv-
ing that voice as soon as it speaks.

But which chemistry could hand us over the process through
which this *auflösen* slides much further in the system and in the
texts? In the *Philosophy of Religion*, for example, and more precisely,
in "Absolute Religion": "The resolution of the contradiction is the
concept, a resolution which the understanding does not attain because it starts from the presupposition that the two [distinguished
moments] both are and remain utterly independent of each
other."[3] Yet later in the same book, concerning being posited as a
determination of the concept, one finds: "The concept is different
from Being, and the peculiar quality of the difference lies in this
that the Notion absorbs and abolishes it [*sie aufhebt*]."[4]

Two words brush against each other; the same text is written
with the two of them, between the two, in the thickness of a
shadow or in the calculation [*calcul*] of an infinitesimal difference.
It is probably through the *Aesthetics* that the movement of the
combined or the blurred writing of the *auflösen* and of the
aufheben is most accentuated.[5] If, at the beginning of the
Aesthetics, art is described as "one of the means which dissolve . . .
the . . . opposition" (*A*, 1:56) whose moments Hegel has just recalled in order to crown them with the opposition between theory and determinate being [*être-là*], and if this dissolution in art
amounts to "bring back," the opposition to "unity" (ibid.), at the

end of the *Aesthetics*, when art is itself dissolved and is ready for the philosophical sublation that is announced from the outset—and from the dissolution of the opposition in art—it looks at though, in one of its last sentences, the absolute were mistaken about a word: "the presence and agency of the Absolute no longer appears positively unified with the characters and aims of the real world but asserts itself only in the negative form of cancelling everything not correspondent with it, and subjective personality alone shows itself self-confident and self-assured at the same time *in this dissolution [Auflösung]*."[6]

It is no longer a question of chemistry—or else, it is a question of the strange and unsublatable chemistry of a text that mixes up its words or rather (and one might then have to speak of pathology) of a text that lets its words be contaminated or be shaken by each other, or make each other go bad, be *both* sublated and dissolved. By giving oneself over to the chance of happy finds in language, one always risks this kind of contamination; one always risks heterogeneous combinations. By speaking in water, and by wishing to be heard in it, one risks making words only murmur [*bruisser*]. One always risks letting oneself be caught unawares by a *Witz*, and the delight that speculative thought at times experiences always risks being carried away in some voluptuous debauchery.

The Remark of the *aufheben* might thus simultaneously consti-tute the entire program of a speculative language, of its vocabulary and of its syntax, *and*, among the very dispositions of this program, as a piece of its "naïve machinery," the permanent risk—that is, a risk *having always already taken place*—of a *witzig* accident. An ac-cident that represents both, and paradoxically (but in Hegelian logic, what is a para-dox [*para-doxe*]?), the success—somehow un-expected—of speculation as verbal speculation (or as a speculative Verb, a *Witz* whose name is Logos) *and* the unsettling of this spec-ulation, its falling in again with pleasure (or desire: *Lust*), with ex-citement, its ruin in heterogeneousness and in frivolity, its dispersion in the "infinitely wide field of witty and striking notions . . ." (*A*, 1:398). The chance of speculative thought, that is, the chance of the concept as much as that of language, is itself—if one dare say so, in the being-chance of its chance [*dans l'être-chance de sa chance*]—formed *right at the level* of its form. That is, it is formed right at the level of this torsion that constitutes its form so as to carry along, if ever it arises fortunately in a word, not *only* the dialectical loss of its gain (which is always, in this case, the gain of a loss) but *also*, and in spite of its *meaning* as of its will, an "accident" between loss and gain. This accident no longer has the nature of "accidentality," no discourse can measure its occurrence or its repercussions [*l'événement ni la portée*]—so much so that it is even no longer calculable in the way that a differential coefficient [*dérivée*] or a play on words both are. But it is nevertheless what the *Science of Logic* had irresistibly, necessarily, discreetly to "account" for as its text.

It is therefore altogether an ultimate surprise—as it were, an inevitable chance—and a logical conclusion to find somewhere, in an Addition to Hegel's discourse, a (badly) chosen place for this incalculable. In the commentary on the notions of possibility and of contingency in § 145 of the *Encyclopedia*, Hegel went so far as to say:

Contingency . . . as a form of the Idea as a whole . . . deserves its due. . . . For example, although language is the body of thinking, as it were [*gleichsam*], still chance indisputably [*unbedenklich*—but it is also "without reflecting" or "without thinking"] plays a decisive [*entschieden*] role in it [*Rolle*]. . . . It is quite correct to say that the task of science and, more precisely, of philosophy, consists generally in coming to know the necessity that is hidden under the semblance of contingency; but this must not be understood to mean that contingency pertains only to our subjective views and that it must therefore be set aside totally if we wish to attain the truth. Scientific endeavours which one-sidedly push in this direction will not escape the justified reproach of being an empty game [*leere Spielerei*] and a strained pedantry [*steifer Pedantismus*]. (*Enc.*, 1:§ 145:219)

In rereading this text in every sense (in every direction), one will, no doubt, always find it aligned to the science and to the truth that it entitles, but one will also find it resolutely irreducible to what the concept—and not the text—of speculation can mean. It is indeed—to mention only this feature among others—not a specular or a dialectical syntax that adjoins the contingency of language to its necessity but the "although" [*obschon*] of an oppositive or a disjunctive syntax. Hegel, however, will nevertheless remain the one who elsewhere quotes the French *Witz*: "La vérité, en la repoussant, on l'embrasse."[7] But truth here is not so much pushed away as disturbed or displaced, one knows not where. Chance must not be reduced to necessity; this gesture would be "unilateral": a certain chance thus plays the game of the speculative, the game of the *aufheben*. And as if by chance, language is a remarkable case of it. There is no verbal speculation because there is speculative chance in language—or because the speculative spirit of language is contingent, which also means that the "body of thought" itself is contingent. *Aufheben* is the form, the statement of speculation, because its contingency is a "form of the Idea." As if one finally learned what is at issue with the "plastic exposition," that is with the text of the *aufheben*: the speculative *Darstellung* is *itself* contingent, itself hazardous [*hasardeuse*].

Admittedly, the most constraining necessity requires that the absolute hand itself over to the empirical determinate being [*être-là*], that it pass through and as this contingency. The *chance of forms* is thus its truth. But one also sees that this other necessity insinuates itself in the passage, as an inevitable accident—a happy surprise and a rupture (or an excrescence) of the speculative ring. Not to mention the gap that is produced unexpectedly through the passage. *Chance deforms.*

Hegel's text, then, held by the necessity of taking its chance, has continually broken here and there, haphazardly, in Additions or in Remarks, the course of its own meaning [*sens*], in order subtly, tortuously to seize a chance that might no longer be the reverse of the necessary [*du nécessaire*]—and it has not been possible to achieve this without leaving some traces, incised or in relief, in the irregularity of a logical syntax, or in the unsettling of the lexicon.

Later in the *Encyclopedia* Hegel notes other cases of this contingency that plays a "decisive role " (which does not mean "determinate"). First of all, monsters: "the impotence of Nature to adhere strictly to the Notion in its realization . . . blurs the essential limits of species and genera by intermediate and defective forms, which continually furnish counter examples to every fixed distinction, this even occurs within a specific genus, that of man, for example, where monstrous births, on the one hand, must be considered as belonging to the genus . . ." (*Enc. II*, § 250:24). Or in note, and with a polemical verve: "Herr Krug once challenged the Philosophy of Nature to perform the feat of deducing *only* his pen. One could perhaps give him hope that *his* pen would have the glory of being deduced, if ever philosophy should advance so far and have such a clear insight into every great theme in heaven and on earth, past and present, that there was nothing more important to comprehend."[8]

An author's pen cannot be deduced. The pen with which one writes *Remark: The Expression "Aufheben"* does not quite let itself be conceived. It is monstrous. It writes in spite of everything—but it is also always in danger of not being able to write in a certain way. It has happened to Hegel: "I have long doubted whether I should write to you, since everything written or spoken again depends solely on explanation; or since I feared explanation, which once embarked upon is so dangerous" (Hegel to his fiancée, Nuremberg, summer 1811).[9]

The Speculative Unrest
(1999)

To see the translation of a book appear twenty-eight years after it has been published in its original language (and after the publication of many other books, often already translated into English) can only be disquieting. To what extent does one still agree with the book? And what can be revealed to the author by the demands of translation, which can sometimes be severe, indeed cruel, according to its justified requirements (and such will have been those of Céline Surprenant, to whom I here express my gratitude, and who in fact will have unburdened the text of heavinesses that English would not have allowed)?

I must admit that in this book there were youthful mistakes that were partly also those of an epoch: a certain stylistic and lexical complication, joined to an immoderate taste for exploiting all the resources of language, manifest as much in the appeal to French as in the constant recourse to German (showing a permanent reticence to *translate* . . . , in the name of the wealth of each language). In fact, this epoch was discovering that one does not philosophize outside language and that the body of the latter is also the flesh of thought. But the Hegelian question that is stirred in these pages has to do with nothing else: this is why, without seeking to excuse the mistakes of an effervescent age, I do not have to take too much distance from this book.

I note, on the contrary, how much it was already preoccupied with a motif that has since become the theme of another book on Hegel: unrest [*inquiétude*]. I did not know that this motif had appeared twenty-eight years earlier (yet I have known for some time that one always rewrites one's book, as Borges once said . . .). Someone had to draw my attention to it.[1] I had to face the fact: toward the middle of the analysis (in Chapter 4), unrest [*Unruhe*] plays a decisive role. The sentence that might best summarize the concern of the book is the one that states that "Unrest is neither the name or the nickname of the aufheben: it makes it restless,"[2] or, to be more precise, that "agitation makes the *Aufhebung* restless" (agitation is one of the meanings of *Unruhe*, just as it is the primary meaning of unrest, unquietness [*inquiétude*]). That is to say that the rapid and incessant movement that goes simultaneously for and against the "proposition" in order to achieve "speculation" and, more generally, goes for and against language in order to reach thought, in order to free thought *from* language but *in* language, that this movement, then, troubles the sovereign power of the *Aufhebung*, disrupts the essential mainspring of the system, and therefore makes the system restless, makes it anxious, drives it wild, prevents absolute knowledge from absolutizing itself.

Now, it is indeed this unrest that gives Hegel's text its greatness and its strength. Simultaneously, he immobilizes and exhausts the entire effort of thought in a sort of enormous tautology of the concept (and it is in this way that it has become banal to call

"Hegelian" everything in thought that seems closed, satisfied, and imperialist), *and* (that is to say *but* . . .), he stirs, shakes, renders unstable this tautology and ceaselessly relaunches its *logos* in the desperate flight of its own meaning [*sens*] and its own truth.

But this flight is that of the True or of the Good such as the System appeared to have posited them. It is not a flight toward an always more remote horizon, toward an interminable accomplishment: it rather means that the True and the Good are *already there*, already accomplished *hic et nunc*, but their accomplishment is the *Unruhe* itself, and thus the eternal return (if it is permitted to link Hegel and Nietzsche!) of the effort of thought that is its own meaning [*qui est à lui-même son sens*].

The presence of this thought in Hegel was recently noted in a book by Michael Turnheim, where a chapter devoted to the confrontation between Hegel and Freud concerning the *Witz* refers, among others, to *The Speculative Remark*. It seemed that nothing was more appropriate than to append this chapter from a book published twenty-six years after my own and written in an entirely other horizon, thus witnessing encounters and crossings that form the contingent but continuous course of the work of thought.

Appendix

Extract from Michael Turnheim, *Das Andere im Gleichen: Über Trauer, Witz, und Politik* (Stuttgart, Klett & Cotta, 1999), chap. 2, pt. 6.

The Linguistic Advances of Chance

In a surprising way, it is precisely Hegel, to whom the "puritanical condemnation of the *Witz*"[1] falls, who will provide us with the means to enlighten what remains uncertain in Freud, as far as the relation between the *Witz* and knowledge is concerned. Although Hegel states that it is the task of knowledge "to overcome" [*überwinden*] chance, he states the following: "In respect of Mind and its works, just as in the case of Nature, we must guard against being so far misled by a well-meant endeavour after rational knowledge [*Erkenntnis*], as to try to exhibit the necessity of phenomena which are marked by a decided contingency, or, as the phrase is, to construe *a priori*" (*Enc. I*, § 145:206). What resists knowledge cannot simply be imputed to "the impotence of Nature to adhere strictly to the concept" (*Enc. II*, § 250:24), a powerlessness that the existence of "monsters" [*Missgeburten*] attests. Neither did Hegel content himself with the idea that one ought to "let chance be" [*den Zufall sein zu lassen*],[2] since he knew that chance—"for example," he says, as if he wanted immediately to restrict the worrying character of his observation—also affects the very "body" [*Leib*] of thought:

Although language is the body of thinking, as it were, still chance indisputably plays a decisive role in it, and the same is true with regard to the configurations of law, art, etc. It is quite correct to say that the task of science and, more precisely, of philosophy, consists generally in coming to know the necessity that is hidden under the semblance of contingency; but this must not be understood to mean that contingency pertains only to our subjective views, and that it must therefore be set aside totally if we wish to attain the truth. Scientific endeavours which one-sidedly push in this direction will not escape the justified reproach of being an empty game and a strained pedantry [*einer leeren Spielerei und eines steifen Pedantismus nicht entgehen*]. (*Enc. I*, § 145:219)

The expression "empty game" [*leere Spielerei*], which one would have expected among Hegel's contemptuous remarks on the *Witz*, is here, on the contrary, linked to a thought distinguished by its "strained pedantry," that is to say, to its lack of *Witz*. At the same time, the word *although* at the beginning of the passage refers us to the importance of the danger— the presence of contingency not only in nature but also at the very place of "speculative thought," where dialectics is supposed to transform contingency into necessity.[3] Yet Hegel does not wish at all to suppress such a contingency affecting the "body of thought"—on the contrary, he believes that it is "a delight . . . to find in the language words which [thanks to their *precise* 'double meaning' (*Doppelsinn*)] have in themselves a speculative meaning" (*SL*, 107).[4] The twofold meaning of *Aufhebung*, essential for the Hegelian concept [*Auffassung*], shows that such a contingency is situated at the *heart* of the system. But Hegel here still takes an additional and decisive step—his undertaking is not limited to the *heart* nor to a *precise* twofold meaning.[5] For even if linguistic contingencies arising in the *Witz*—"which . . . to our astonishment, combin[es] things that are poles apart from each other" (*A*, 1:407)—threaten to contaminate the entire system and have to be rejected, nothing must escape "sublation" [*Aufhebung*]. This is why—as Jean-Luc Nancy has impressively shown—in order to save itself, the system of the *Aufhebung* can only play *as a whole* with its own "dissolution" [*Auflösung*][6]—and this, through its *Witz*, even if Hegel does not quite put it in this way.[7] As soon as one recognizes that language itself, according to its ideal, has something of a "monster," the "monsters" of the world (broadly speaking: the singular events) that resist knowledge can escape the rejection to which they would otherwise be destined [*vorgesehenen*].[8]

There might thus be a disquieting [*unheimlich*] and unavowed proximity between Hegel's "speculative thought" and the *Witz*. It is precisely what allows us, against the current of Hegel's historicizing tendency, to detach the *Witz* from the regressive sphere where it remains caught in Freud. As the etymology, which refers the word *Witz* to the root *Wissen*, indicates,[9] the play on words of the *Witz* that Freud rightly links to the "linguistic advances [*sprachliches Entgegenkommen*]"[10] of chance or to the "chance possibilities which thus arise" in language is less the matter of psychology than of the relation to knowledge.[11] What Freud says of the two aspects of the play at work in "word-associations" [*Wortwitz*]—"relief from psychical expenditure that is already there and economizing in psychical expenditure that is only about to be called for" (*SE*, 8:127)—does not apply only to the child or to what remains of childhood but also and especially to knowledge ("speculative thought") itself. The "act of recognition" (*SE*, 8:121) should encounter its limit in contingency. But, thanks to the contingency of language itself (the condition of the "replacement of thing-associations by word-associations and the use of absurdity" (*SE*, 8:127), contingency, instead of being excluded, can be admitted in the text (which henceforth becomes spiritual).[12] To paraphrase Freud—what knowledge would have wished to economize (by excluding what escapes it), will yet be "sublated" through the "relief" from the constraints at work in language.[13]

Thus, that "the Good, the absolutely Good, . . . need not wait upon us, but is already by implication, as well as in full actuality, accomplished"[14] would appear to arise in the Witz-language that is fortunately not ideal, and that was (as "monster") ready to make advances to chance from the start. In the Witz-language the Good, however, turns out to be less the presence of Redemption through absolute knowledge than the possibility of catching a brief glimpse of its impossibility.[15]

Notes

"Speaking in Water"

I am very grateful to Jean-Luc Nancy for his willingness to discuss the text and the translation of *La remarque spéculative* at various stages of the process. I would also like to thank friends and colleagues who helped me to carry the work through, Stanford University Press editors Helen Tartar and Larry Goldsmith, and copyeditor Joe Abbott.

1. J.-L. Nancy, *Hegel, L'inquiétude du négatif* (Paris: Hachette, 1997).

2. J.-L. Nancy, *Le discours de la syncope: I. Logodaedalus* (Paris: Aubier-Flammarion, 1976), 9; "La décision d'existence," in *Une pensée finie* (Paris: Galilée, 1990), translated by B. Holmes et al. as "The Decision of Existence," in J.-L. Nancy, *The Birth to Presence* (Stanford, Calif.: Stanford University Press, 1993), 97.

3. Nancy, *Hegel, L'inquiétude du négatif*, 51.

4. W. Hamacher, "Ou, séance, touche de Nancy, ici," *Paragraph* 16, no. 2 (1993): 229. A special issue titled *On the Work of Jean-Luc Nancy*, edited by Peggy Kamuf.

5. See, among others, Nancy, *Birth to Presence*, 396 n. 12; Kamuf, "On the subject of ravishment (*À même* Jean-Luc Nancy)," *Paragraph* 16, no. 2 (1993): 211; R. Gasché, "Alongside the Horizon," in *On Jean-Luc Nancy: The Sense of Philosophy*, edited by D. Sheppard, S. Sparks, and C. Thomas (London: Routledge, 1997), 144; *Hegel After Derrida*, edited by S. Barnett (London: Routledge, 1996), 318 n. 7.

6. Nancy, *Hegel, L'inquiétude du négatif*, 51. For a short review of this book, see *Bulletin de littérature hégélienne XII, Archives de Philosophie* 62, no. 3 (1999): 31.

7. See *RS*, 28, 49, 81, 103, 106, 142.

8. S. Monod, preface to J. Conrad, *Typhoon*, translated by A. Gide (1918; édition bilingue, Paris: Gallimard, 1991), 25.

9. On the *Witz*, see Nancy, "Menstruum Universale," in *Birth to Presence*, 248–65.

10. Nancy, *Hegel, L'inquiétude du négatif*, 55.

11. See Preamble, note 17.

12. See Chap. 4. Nancy indicates on two occasions that his commentary on Hegel should be referred back to Heidegger with a view to exploring the motif of epiphany (See Chap. 1, note 13, and Chap. 6, note 1).

13. See D. Kambouchner's review of *The Speculative Remark*, "Le labyrinthe de la présentation," *Critique* 34 (1978): 41–62.

14. Nancy, *Le discours de la syncope*, 13.

15. J.-L. Nancy, *Ego sum* (Paris: Flammarion, 1979).

16. One could study the issue of the text and of reading in Nancy in order to distinguish it from other "problematics of textuality" in the vein of Rodolphe Gasché's enlightening analysis of Jacques Derrida's and Paul de Man's conceptions of the text and of reading. To put it briefly, what is at issue is the kind of knowledge that *reading* makes possible. Gasché argues convincingly that what makes these two approaches incompatible is their treatment of "difference" (between "*logos* and *mythos*, concept and metaphor, philosophy and sophistics"), which the former allows but the latter denies. See R. Gasché, "Giving to Read" and "Adding Oddities," in *The Wild Card of Reading: On Paul de Man* (Cambridge, Mass.: Harvard University Press, 1998), 149–81. In the case of Nancy the study of the *question of the text* might begin by reckoning with the way the question of the text is soon relayed by the *question du sens*, as the work on *interpretation* in Heidegger (*Le partage des voix* [Paris: Galilée, 1982], 39, 64 n. 45) marks, just as by the other motifs throughout Nancy's subsequent work, which sometimes seem to do without any reference to the *text*. But this does not mean that the set of preoccupations that the *text* in the early work signals simply disappears, and the analysis of this question would therefore consist of exploring this "modification." Notwithstanding the fact that it involves, even if anecdotally, *The Speculative Remark*, it might

be useful to refer to a recent interview where, asked about the concept of "excrit," Nancy replies:

> It is a word which has occurred to me in reaction to a craze for writing, the text, salvation through literature, etc. There is a sentence from Bataille: "Language alone indicates the sovereign moment where it no longer has any currency." It is my daily prayer. He means: there is assuredly only language, but what language indicates, is non-language, the things themselves. . . . This reminds me of a very early meeting with Ricoeur, at his home in Châtenay. He had just read my first book on Hegel and, after opening the garden door, said: "This is all very well, but what about the garden in all that?" I have never forgotten: the "excrit" is the garden, the fact that writing indicates its own [*propre*] outside, is decanted and shows things. ("Le partage, l'infini et le jardin," *Libération*, February 17, 2000)

On the concept of "excrit" see "Excription," in Nancy, *Birth to Presence*, 319–40; *Corpus* (Paris: Métailié, 1992).

17. J.-L. Nancy (with Philippe Lacoue-Labarthe), *L'absolu littéraire: Théorie de la littérature du romantisme allemand* (Paris: Seuil, 1978), translated by P. Barnard and C. Lester as *The Literary Absolute: The Theory of Literature in German Romanticism* (Albany: State University of New York Press, 1987). For references to related works, see *Paragraph* 16, no. 2 (1993): 232–38.

18. "Entr'acte," preface to J.-M. Galay, *Philosophie et invention textuelle: Essai sur la poétique d'un texte kantien* (Paris: Klincksieck, 1977), ix.

The Speculative Remark

1. By bracketing the saying Nancy appeals to the assonance between "deux mots" and "deux maux" (two evils) as in the French maxim: "de deux maux, il faut choisir le moindre." "Il fallait donc se décider, entre des mots": *mots* here also denotes a "witty" saying.—Trans.

2. It is true that in the *Phenomenology* (*PS*, 138), the *meaning* [*sens*] of which Hegel speaks is that of a consciousness and not that of a word.

Chapter 1

1. A. Koyré, "Note sur la langue et la terminologie hégéliennes," in *Études d'histoire et de la pensée philosophique*, 2d ed. (Paris: Gallimard, 1971), 191–224.

2. J. Hyppolite, *Logique et existence: Essai sur la logique de Hegel* (Paris: P.U.F., 1953), translated by L. Lawlor and A. Sen as *Logic and Existence* (Albany: State University of New York Press, 1997).

3. W. Marx, *Absolute Reflexion und Sprache* (Frankfurt am Main: Klosterman, 1967).

4. J. Derrida, "De l'économie restreinte à l'économie générale. Un hégélianisme sans réserve," in *L'écriture et la différence* (Paris: Seuil, 1967), translated by A. Bass as "From Restricted to General Economy: A Hegelianism Without Reserve," in *Writing and Difference* (London: Routledge and Kegan Paul, 1978), 251–77; J. Derrida, "Le puits et la pyramide. Introduction à la sémiologie de Hegel," in *Marges de la philosophie* (Paris: Minuit, 1972), translated by A. Bass as "The Pit and the Pyramid: Introduction to Hegel's Semiology," in *Margins of Philosophy* (Brighton: Harvester Press, 1982), 69–108.

5. An *almanac*, if we are to believe (and why not?) Egyptian etymology, is a *calculation for memory* [calcul pour la mémoire]. We will therefore see that something of the almanac will *also* be at issue.

6. There exist literary examples of it—such as that of Heine, which must be retranscribed as an apologue of what the story of a "mot" on the *Aufhebung* could be—of a "bon mot" or of a silence, as we shall see: "Nature," Hegel once told me, "is very odd; the very instruments that she uses for the most sublime ends, she also uses them for the dirtiest work, such as for example, that organ to which the highest mission is entrusted, the reproduction of humanity, also serves the purpose . . ." (*Ludwig Börne*, 4th Book, in *Beiträge zur deutschen Ideologie* [Frankfurt am Main: Ullstein, 1971], 342). We know that the same narrator has reported the last word (Kierkegaard has quoted it): "When Hegel was on his deathbed, he said: 'There is only one who has understood me.' But he quickly added ill-humoredly: 'And he did not understand me either' " (*Zur Geschichte der Religion und Philosophie in Deutschland*, III, 84).

7. Incidentally, has this work of thematic and thetic commentary not been done and redone for a long time? There is indeed no great study on Hegel that is not a study on the *Aufhebung*, and for a very good reason. Curiously, however, to our knowledge, there exists no "specific" developed study of this concept or of its word—not even in the work of H. Niel, *De*

la médiation dans la philosophie de Hegel (Paris: Aubier, 1945), in that of J. van der Meulen, *Hegel: Die gebrochene Mitte* (Hamburg: F. Meiner, 1958), or in that of T. Bodammer, *Hegels Deutung der Sprache: Interpretationen zu Hegels Äusserungen über die Sprache* (Hamburg: F. Meiner, 1969), where one might have expected it. Nor is there anything concerning the *Aufhebung* in G. Lebrun, *La patience du concept: Essai sur le discours hégélien* (Paris: Gallimard, 1972), whose perspicaciousness and attention to Hegelian language are curiously and as if meticulously converted into another discourse *on* Hegel rather than into a crossing [*traversée*] *of* his text. There, as elsewhere, and no doubt according to an implacable Hegelian law, one *turns*, in every sense of the word, *around* the *Aufhebung*. (Even so, one should distinguish two ways of turning around: for French authors, the double meaning [*sens*] of *aufheben* is a foreign curiosity, which one respects by avoiding it, unless one tackles the problem of its translation (as Koyré has done, and then Derrida, for whom the equivalent *relève* is not a mere translation but rather the affirmation of the problem of translation. One obviously cannot stop at the verb *sursumer*, coined by J.-J. Labarrière and G. Jarczyk in their translation of the *Science of Logic* [*La science de la logique* (Paris: Aubier, 1972)], which entails at least two mistakes: wanting to translate and to speak a philosophical *Kunstsprache*, to which Hegel will oblige us to go back . . .); for German authors, *aufheben* can be avoided insofar as the word and its meaning are familiar, that is, according to Hegel, insofar as the "thoughtless habit" presides over the use of the "mother tongue" (School Address, September 29, 1809—see below, Chap. 4). (Just before the completion of this translation, at the end of 1999, I received a DEA dissertation [the equivalent of a master's thesis] submitted to Université de Paris I by M. Nicolas Coulon, titled "The Debates Around the French Translations of the Hegelian Term *Aufhebung*." It consists of an exhaustive inquiry on the history of these translations and a critical analysis of all the adopted solutions [including, therefore, a critique of *The Speculative Remark*], and it concludes by proposing a new translation, namely the neologism *surlever* [literally, *overlifting*]. I replied to the author that another neologism can, on the one hand, only aggravate the problem and that, on the other hand, his work leads one all the more to think that Hegel's operation on the word *Aufhebung* is already itself an operation of translation or of translation within his own language [or on its limits], which forbids us to think of "translating" this term into another language. This is why I still think today that Derrida's proposal of an "equivalence"—rather than a "translation"—in the French verb *relever* remains, in my language, the best possible course.—J.-L. N.)

8. The English translations of Hegel are modified according to Jean-Luc Nancy's specific inflections of Hegel's text, which he quotes from the *Phänomenologie des Geistes*, edited by Hoffmeister (Hamburg: F. Meiner, 1952), and *La phénoménologie de l'esprit*, 2 vols., translated by Jean Hyppolite (Paris: Montaigne, 1941).—Trans.

9. This is why we have left aside some of its articulations, including its articulation in the text of the Preface as a whole.

10. Without, however, pleading guilty, that is, without having here recourse to the power of the negative. Philosophical writing is here *presented* [*darstellt*]; it is not quite *sublated*. This text is disreputable. We will have to come back to this particular logic and to the Hegelian topoi where it circulates: first of all, as we see, to philosophy as it is written and it is read [*en tant qu'elle s'écrit et se lit*].

11. Let us not forget that, for Hegel, *plastisch* necessarily has the twofold value of plasticity (that of a "plastic exposition," where one gives up the rigidity of individual thoughts, of the *Meinungen* [cf. *SL*, 40] and of plastic beauty [cf. sculpture in *Aesthetics*]). The latter is, more particularly, characteristic of Socrates' nature, to whom we will have to come back, and of the young men Plato presents (*dichtet*, to compose, to write up [*rédiger*]) in his dialogues (*LHP*, 1:402). Now, it is impossible to imagine being able today (1831) to write dialogues with such characters, and "still less could one count on readers of such disposition" (*SL*, 40).

12. In the phrase "milieu de manifestation," *milieu* is used in the biological sense of what surrounds and influences a living organism, such as the *milieu de culture* where cells are allowed to grow, and in the social sense of "environment." But it also denotes an intermediary term, state, or position. Although retaining something of the biological sense of *milieu*, the phrase *l'être-milieu du milieu* refers to the series of terms in Hegel that are related to the process of mediation: *die Mitte* (the middle,

the middle term), *mittelbar* (mediate, indirect), *vermitteln* (to achieve union, to mediate, to bring about), *Vermittelheit* (mediatedness). Hence it is here also translated as "the middle." See M. Inwood, *A Hegel's Dictionary* (Oxford: Blackwell, 1992), 183–86.—Trans.

13. To recall, it is necessarily to recall the Heideggerian commentary on the introduction to the *Phenomenology*, where the term *epiphany* entails the rigorous logic we just recalled. See M. Heidegger, *Hegels Phänomenologie des Geistes* (Frankfurt am Main: Klosterman, 1980), translated by P. Emad and K. Maly as *Hegel's Phenomenology of Spirit* (Bloomington: Indiana University Press, 1988). The present study depends on that commentary in its entirety insofar as it might form, on a small scale, a sort of lining of it [*doublure*] by focusing on the motif of the language of epiphany, that is, on a motif that is out of line [*décalé*]—which is also that of a certain "gap" [*décalage*] in Hegel's text of which Heidegger does not speak. One might as well say that one should also reread Heidegger, the Heideggerian text in general, and the role that Hegel might be playing in it. This, however, is another matter, which is undertaken in Ph. Lacoue-Labarthe's "L'oblitération," *Critique* 29 (1973).

14. One can also say, more precisely, that this hermeneutical constraint prescribes a certain *presentation* (in the ordinary or literary sense of the term) of philosophical writing, since the discourse of philosophy is essentially given to *read*, taking its place among books in general, in literature in the broadest sense—that is, in the field of the category "literature"—whose determination no doubt entails that of a *philosophical literature* as such, contemporary to the modern times of philosophy (that is to say, contemporary to the joint structure of the transcendental illusion) and of hermeneutics, as Paul Ricoeur has drawn it out through his work—cf. the conclusion to *Finitude et culpabilité* (Paris: Aubier, 1960) and bk. 1, chap. 7 of *De l'interprétation: Essai sur Freud* (Paris: Seuil, 1965), translated by D. Savage as *Freud and Philosophy: An Essay on Interpretation* (New Haven, Conn.: Yale University Press, 1970)—and rigorously related it to the philosophy of modern times. It might be useful to give at least a few examples of this hermeneutical presentation—or what could be called the prefatory circle of the philosophical book: In the preface to *Les méditations* in *Oeuvres philosophiques II*, edited by F. Alquié (Paris:

Dunod, 1996), Descartes points in advance to the reader for whom his work is intended: "viamque sequor . . . tam parum tritam, atque ab usu communi tam remotam, ut non utile putarim ipsam in gallico et passim ab omnibus legendo scripto fusius docere, ne debiliora etiam ingenia credere possent eam sibi esse ingrediendam." (One sees that one had to quote the Latin: the translation of the preface will be done by Clerselier only after Descartes's death in 1661, and it would have been somewhat incoherent to uncover that text to the reader of the French translation of the *Meditations*, even though Descartes would have approved of it. Here is the translation: "The route which I follow . . . is so untrodden and so remote from the normal way, that I thought it would not be helpful to give a full account of it in a book written in French and designed to be read by all and sundry, in case weaker intellects might believe that they ought to set out on the same path.")—And that reader must be such as to be already informed of at least the first exercise of meditation, whose reading he will undertake (that is, in this case, the practice too): ". . . I would not urge anyone to read this book except those who are able and willing to meditate seriously with me, and to withdraw their minds from the senses and from all preconceived opinions. Such readers, as I well know, are few and far between."—Unless he should bring into play a strange neutrality of the first reading so as to allow reading: "I therefore ask my readers not to pass judgement on the *Meditations* until they have been kind enough to read through all these objections and my replies to them" (*Meditations on First Philosophy*, vol. 2 of *The Philosophical Writings of Descartes*, translated by J. Cottingham, R. Stoothoff, and D. Murdoch [Cambridge: Cambridge University Press, 1985], 6–8). In Kant's preface to the first edition of *Kritik der reinen Vernunft*, edited by J. Timmermann (Hamburg: F. Meiner, 1998), translated and edited by P. Guyer and A. W. Wood as *Critique of Pure Reason* (Cambridge: Cambridge University Press, 1998), Kant confers upon his reader two simultaneous roles (given first of all, here too, that "this work could never be made suitable for popular use" [A xviii, 104]), the first of which is presented [*mis en scène*] by means of the most constant metaphor of the critique itself, or of reason: "Here I expect from my reader the patience and impartiality of a *judge*" (A xxi, 105). The second role, which is accompanied by a yield of pleasure, is a substitute [*auxiliariat*] in the edification of the system: "It can, as it seems to me, be no small inducement for the reader to unite his effort with that of the author, when he has the prospect of carrying out, according to the outline given above, a great and important piece of work, and that in a complete and lasting way" (A xix, 104).—What is at issue is a hermeneutics of seduction, if one dare say so, that incites one to undertake a reading-writing [*lecture-écriture*] of the critique of the *Critique* and that goes so far as to solicit, in the second preface, the contribution of the reader to the literary completion of the book, as, this time, a yield of pleasure of the system itself (a yield of pleasure that, as we will show elsewhere, relates to the text of the three *Critiques* considered together):

Any philosophical treatise may find itself under pressure in particular passages (for it cannot be as fully armored as a mathematical treatise), while the whole structure of the system, considered as a unity, proceeds without the least danger; . . . Meanwhile, if a theory is really durable, then in time the effect of action and reaction, which at first seemed to threaten it with great danger, will serve only to polish away its rough spots, and if men of impartiality, insight, and true popularity make it their business to do this, then in a short time they will produce even the required elegance. (B xlvi, 123–24).

—Finally, and to present only a third example, one finds most of these motifs in the foreword added by J. G. Fichte to the second printing of the first edition of the *Wissenschaftslehre* [The doctrine of science], where they are displaced this time with respect to the agitated protestation that Fichte raises against the premature and "indiscreet" diffusion that has been made of his unfinished book (it had indeed to be "published as a manuscript for the use of my listeners" and thus not easily legible):

What follows is aimed only for honorable persons and makes sense only for them. . . . I am far from finishing the construction, and I can at this point only invite the public to undertake the future construction with me. Before being able to determine a single proposition with any precision, it will have to be understood on the basis of the whole and [one must] first get a general view of it. . . . Any philosophy is entitled to expect from its reader that it follow the thread of the reasoning. (My translation, from the French translation by A. Philonenko as *Doctrine de la science* [Paris: J. Vrin, 1980], 14–15.)

Through these examples one can already assess the extent to which the

Preface to the *Phenomenology* belongs, but not only, not exclusively, or simply to the hermeneutical circles of the author and the reader, of the text and its conception, of the preface and the "body" of the book.

15. The coining of *pré-posé* as a synonym of presupposition allows the homonymy with *préposé*, which denotes an employee, an official of customs, a postman, etc.—Trans.

16. The German text reads: "Die eine Weise stört die andere, und erst diejenige philosophische Exposition würde es erreichen, plastisch zu sein, welche streng die Art des gewöhnlichen Verhältnisses der Teile eines Satzes ausschlösse. . . . Daß die Form des Satzes aufgehoben wird, muß nicht nur auf. . . ." (Only a philosophical exposition that rigidly excludes the usual way of relating the parts of a proposition could achieve the goal of plasticity. . . .)—Trans.

17. It is hardly surprising to find that this program is already inscribed in the course of a text by Jacques Derrida: "I emphasize the Hegelian *Aufhebung*, such as it is interpreted by a certain Hegelian discourse, for it goes without saying that the double meaning of *Aufhebung* could be written otherwise" (*Positions* [Paris: Minuit, 1972], translated and annotated by A. Bass as *Positions* [London: Athlone Press, 1987], 41). It is the text of an interview, and on this account, no doubt, it is more than any other the concern of the order of discourse (of propositions). One does not know, therefore, what it would mean to take it literally [*le prendre à sa lettre*]. This sentence moreover systematically depends on the formula concerning Hegel in *Of Grammatology*: "first thinker of writing"—whose word "thinker" would deserve a remark analogous to the one that we will make concerning "self" [*soi*] and "meaning" [*sens*]. But one could ask: why, then, simply not have started from this program? First of all, for the simple reason that one never carries out someone else's program, however much one owes to it, and by wishing to do so, one has never produced anything but the sad effects of the Schools [*les tristes effets des écoles*]. But also, and above all, because of the singular Hegelian game [*partie*] that is played out in this sentence by Derrida, if one should take it literally. For by writing that something should go "without saying" [*de soi*] and that what should be at issue is a "double meaning," Derrida himself takes up the very Hegelian position that he claims to exceed in the same sentence.

And, even more, that one should be able to point to "*a certain* Hegelian discourse," and, consequently, to evoke in this way at least *another* discourse, no less Hegelian, or of Hegel, sends us to an alterity that one ought to try to read in Hegel's text. If there is here good reason for repeating Derrida, it is because he repeats Hegel or because something of Hegel—(in Hegel)—repeats (itself): we are therefore taking the risk of having to repeat (ourselves), but it might be Hegel who commits us to repeat this repetition. . . . In brief, if we had to recall that the School is sad, one sees that all this, on the other hand, could very well take a comical turn. But let us not be too much in a hurry. (Let us add that this work was presented in March 1973 at Jacques Derrida's Seminar at the École Normale Supérieure, rue d'Ulm.)

Chapter 2

1. It might be useful to refer to the German text of this Remark, insofar as we have transcribed it rather than translated it (a *translation* might indeed imply the mastery and the understanding [*intelligence*] of the text, which, on many points, cannot but be lacking, *already within German language*, to a reading still awaiting its *sublation*: in this way, in the following work, we will continually seek the mode of inscription of such a text . . .). Here is the inscription:

Aufheben und das *Aufgehobene* (das *Ideelle*) ist einer des wichtigsten Begriffe der Philosophie, eine Grundbestimmung, die schlechthin allenthalben wiederkehrt, deren Sinn bestimmt aufzufassen und besonders vom *Nichts* zu unterscheiden ist.—Was sich aufhebt, wird dadurch nicht zu Nichts. Nichts ist das *Unmittelbare*; ein Aufgehobenes dagegen ist ein *Vermitteltes*; es ist das Nichtseiende, aber als *Resultat*, das von einem Sein ausgegangen ist. Es hat daher die *Bestimmtheit, aus der es herkommt, noch an sich.*

Aufheben hat in der Sprache den gedoppelten Sinn, daß es so viel als aufbewahren, *erhalten* bedeutet und zugleich so viel als aufhören lassen, *ein Ende machen*. Das Aufbewahren selbst schliesst schon das Negative in sich, daß etwas seiner Unmittelbarkeit und damit einem den äußerlichen Einwirkungen offenen Dasein entnommen wird, um es zu erhalten.—So ist das Aufgehobene ein zugleich Aufbewahrtes, das nur seine Unmittelbarkeit verloren hat, aber darum nicht vernichtet ist.—Die angegebenen zwei Bestimmungen des *Aufhebens* können lexikalisch als zwei *Bedeutungen* dieses Wortes aufgeführt werden. Auffallend müste es aber sein, daß eine Sprache dazu gekommen ist, ein und dasselbe Wort fürt zwei entgegengesetzte Bestimmungen zu gebrauchen. Für das spekulative Denken ist es erfreulich, in der Sprache Wörter zu finden, welche eine spekulative Bedeutung an ihnen selbst haben; die deutsche Sprache hat mehrere dergleichen. Der Doppelsinn des lateinischen: *tollere* (der durch den Ciceronianischen Witz: *tollendum esse Octavium* berühmt geworden) geht nicht so weit; die affirmative Bestimmung geht nur bis zum Emporheben. Etwas ist nur insofern aufgehoben, als es in die Einheit mit seinem Entgegengesetzen getreten ist; in dieser nähern Bestimmung als ein Reflektiertes kann es passend *Moment* genannt werden. *Gewicht* und *Entfernung* von einem Punkt heissen beim Hebel dessen mechanische *Momente* um der *Dieselbigkeit* ihrer Wirkung willen bei aller sonstigen Verschiedenheit eines Reellen, wie das ein Gewicht ist, und eines Ideellen, der bloß räumlichen Bestimmung, der Linie; s. Enzykl. der philos. Wissenschaft, 3te Ausg. § 261 Anm.—Noch öfter wird die Bemerkung sich aufdringen, dass die philosophische Kunstsprache für reflektierte Bestimmungen lateinische Ausdrücke gebraucht, entweder weil die Muttersprache keine Ausdrücke dafür hat, oder wenn sie deren hat, wie hier, weil ihr Ausdruck mehr an das Unmittelbare, die fremde Sprache aber mehr an das Reflektierte erinnert.

Der nähere Sinn und Ausdruck, den Sein und Nichts, indem sie nunmehr *Momente* sind, erhalten, hat sich bei der Betrachtung des Daseins als der Einheit, in der sie aufbewahrt sind zu ergeben. . . . (*Wissenschaft der Logik*, edited by G. Lasson [Hamburg: F. Meiner, 1971], 93–95)

2. Many of Hegel's Remarks have the same ambiguous status—but not all of them, especially in the *Science of Logic*, where a great number of them are "genuine" annexes, which nothing joins to the development as such. The genre of the Remark is not established. We will come back to it later.

3. Even though this annexation is important, it is not exactly exclusive. There is a certain lability in the explicit position of the analysis of the *aufheben* through Hegel's various texts. A "history" of the word in Hegel's works should here be grafted onto the commentary we are undertaking. It would no doubt have to show, among other things, that what is at issue is not a Hegelian *history*—but rather a displacement from text to text. (One could start with the indications given by Jean Wahl in *Le malheur de la conscience* [Paris: Presses Universitaires de France, 1957], 98.) By way of a few points of reference let us note (1) that Hegel's progressive use

of the twofold meaning of *aufheben*, up until the Jena period, should be studied in relation to Schelling's both very close and different use of *aufheben*, which he almost always employs for designating the suppression of difference—it would be a question of working on the relation between *two* differences; (2) that the passage in *Philosophische Propädeutik (1809– 1811)*, Bd. 3 (Stuttgart: Fromann, 1961), translated by A. V. Miller as *The Philosophical Propaedeutic* (Oxford: Blackwell, 1986), § 16 of the Third Lecture, section 2, which, as far as the system is concerned, corresponds to the Remark of the *Science of Logic*, keeps silent on the word *aufheben*, just as any other passages where the term is used do; (3) that the twofold meaning is mentioned in the *Phenomenology of Spirit* at the moment, which can be considered analogous to that of the Remark in the *Science of Logic*, when one passes from "sense certainty" to "perception": "*Sublation* [*Aufheben*] exhibits [*darstellt*] its true twofold meaning which we have seen in the negative: it is at once a *negating* [*Negieren*] and a *preserving*" (68)—but here more than one term (to exhibit, meaning, true) diverges from the text of the *Science of Logic*; (4) that the corresponding passage in *Logic* (*Enc. I*, § 41) is silent on the word but underlines, on the other hand, that the grasping of the concept of the unity being-nothing proceeds from the *speculative proposition*, on which Hegel insists even more in the text of the second edition (now § 88); (5) that concerning § 96 (this time, the second moment of *Dasein*) one finds in the Additions to the *Encyclopedia*, established by Henning and Michelet, the following text:

At this point we should remember [*erinnern*] the double meaning of the German expression [*Ausdruck*] "*aufheben*." On the one hand, we understand it to mean "clear away" [*hinwegräumen*] or "cancel" [*negieren*], and in that sense we say that a law or regulation is cancelled (*aufgehoben*). But the word also means "to preserve" [*aufbewahren*], and we say in this sense that something is well taken care of (*wohl aufgehoben*). This ambiguity in linguistic usage, through which the same word has a negative and a positive meaning, cannot be regarded as an accident or can absolutely not be used as a reason to accuse language of confusion [*Verwirrung*]. We ought rather to recognize here the speculative spirit or our language, which transcends [*hinausschreiten*] the "either-or" of mere understanding (154);

(6) that in other texts, notably in the *Aesthetics*, it often happens that

Hegel (or the notes of his listeners) employs *aufheben* in a context that does not allow for the negative meaning. All these elements at least show a number of variations in the Hegelian text on the *aufheben* (which is therefore not *one*); we will have the opportunity to bring some of them into play.

4. The English translation of the passage suppresses the adverb *schlechthin*: ". . . eine Grundbestimmung, die schlechthin allenthalben wiederkehrt . . ." reads ". . . fundamental determination which repeatedly occurs throughout the whole of philosophy." — Trans.

5. *SL*, 107. Let us note in passing that the remote origin of the common connection and conceptualization (i.e., metaphorization) of the *Aufgehobensein* and of the *Moment* would have to be explored in Hegel's early works on geometry, astronomy, and mechanics (notably, the mechanics of the lever), more particularly, in the theory of proportion developed in the first *Jena Philosophy*. Such an exploration, in itself scholarly, might have to consider the philosophical anteriority and generality of the mathematics of proportions in Hegel . . . , in Descartes, and in Plato.

6. The Hegelian concept of *übergehen* is translated as *passer* in French. Through the past participle of this verb *passé* (as in "c'est qu'il (s')est toujours déjà passé"), a connection is established between the words: the passage, the passing over, the past (*le passé*), as well as *se passer* (to occur, to happen). — Trans.

7. That is admittedly currently done in German. But if, at first, the case is nevertheless here noteworthy (it is not a matter of one of these rather long or accumulative sentences that often prescribe this turn), must we not then here resort, with and in spite of Hegel, to some — speculative? — resource of language?

8. This would go without saying if the *aufheben* were progressively to comprehend and to sublate in itself the *auflösen*. Now, as we just said, this will not be the case — in this text, which will slip from resolution to sublation, nor anywhere else. On the contrary, we will have to recognize later the extent to which and with what ambiguity the *auflösen* comes back to haunt more than one of Hegel's texts. Resolution will also return. But it is too early to speak about it.

9. One can effectively read in that way or the other the last paragraph of the text: "This insight [*Einsicht*]—the sight of the 'empty word' is itself so simple that this beginning as such requires no preparation or further introduction; and, indeed, these preliminary, external reflections [*diese Vorläufigkeit von Räsonnement*] about it were not so much intended to lead up to it [*herbeiführen*] as rather to eliminate all preliminaries" (*SL*, 78).

10. Jacobi, quoted in *SL*, 95–96.

11. This grammatical construction alludes, of course, to Jacques Lacan. It is repeated with the pronominal verb *s'accentuer*, literally, "it accentuates itself."—Trans.

12. After Jacobi's question, a thematic develops around the *accent*, which can be heard, and the verb *accentuer*, which refers, among other things, to pronunciation and sound but which also means "to put an emphasis on something," "to draw out," "to underline." See the earlier use of the expression "to become more pronounced" for *accentuer* that forms part of the thematic of sound and voice that runs throughout the book.—Trans.

13. One therefore comes obviously very near Spinoza's *index sui* of the truth, which "nullo egeat signo" (*De Emendatione* § 36). But without paying attention to it. On quite the contrary—and leaving aside the fact that the Spinozian index might also write—let us say that everything comes from the burying of such an index in the process of a text, of a gesture that here folds this index over a pen—of which we will speak later.

14. Ibid., 104. Infinitesimal calculus is moreover, through a sort of exorbitant privilege, the only particular object whose ulterior analysis Hegel announces in the first chapter of the *Science of Logic*.

15. One no doubt sees that we are reading this relation to differential calculus from a partly different angle than the one adopted by J.-J. Goux ("Dérivable and indérivable," *Critique* 26 [1970], taken up again in *Symbolic Economies: After Marx and Freud* [Ithaca, N.Y.: Cornell University Press, 1990]), who gathers together derivative and *aufheben* in the same economy of *meaning* [*sens*]. We are not however taking issue with Goux's analysis, whose relevance should on the contrary be taken for

granted, here, where one is constantly dealing with the *double* relevance of the *aufheben*.

16. We are thus touching for the second time on what could form the general question of the functioning of the mathematical in philosophy, a question that might itself be accompanied by the singular conjunction of the mathematical and the metaphorical, which would necessitate at least a detour through Kant. We can here only draw attention to this necessary *detour.*—Let us add, as far as Hegel's text is concerned, for clarifying or complicating what is at issue, that the rapprochement between the process of becoming and differential calculus is carried out in a rather equivocal manner. It is not an identity, and it is not a comparison: Hegel states that the one and the other are exposed to the "same dialectic" (in the Aristotelian-Kantian sense, then), which the understanding [*entendement*] opposes (*SL*, 104–5). Their proximity, which is neither conceptual nor rhetorical, entails at least the identity of an effect.

17. Even though it is not so simple, for, as one knows, the "calculus of *fluxions*" was one of the names (one of the metaphors) of infinitesimal calculus.

18. At this point—too late and too early—it becomes necessary to note that the reading here, without respite and in diverse models, comes up against the structure of a text "en abyme" and that the work must in fact obey the constraint of a gigantic Hegelian abyss.—It is, one hopes, so as to observe the strange and double property of this philosophical heraldry, which merges the law of a closure to the unsettling of a meaningless fall. We shall come back to it.

19. In order to point to what could also allow us to develop another analysis, parallel to the one that we are trying to follow, let us note the following: the *aufheben* is expression with respect to meaning and to the concept; considered in itself, it is a word, *Wort*. The Remark says nothing concerning the relation of the expression to the word, that is, nothing about the inside or the content that might come to be expressed in a word (as we already said, we are not dealing with a semiology). It looks as though the *Wort* were by itself likened to the relation of the *Sinn* and of the *Ausdruck*. It might be better, then, to "translate" *Ausdruck* as "sign," if the "sign," taken in itself, has no arbitrariness. . . .

20. Let us also present here the outline of another analysis, which we cannot carry through at the same time as the one we have chosen: the *aufheben* has been understood in the most current sense of "to suppress" only if one forgets the text of the *Phenomenology* mentioned above. In 1812, however, Hegel does not recall the 1807 text. The reader can choose to link or not to link the two texts. But apart from the fact that the "knowledge" ("result") of the first would not solve the problems of the second, we shall see later that the *aufheben* and its "twofold meaning" has been displaced or transformed from one text to the other. This is why we are here choosing to read only the Remark of the *Science of Logic*.

21. One is here no doubt tempted to say that the concept will, after all, be produced later in the *Science of Logic*, when another concept will present exactly the articulation and the properties of the *aufheben* but in a precise determinateness: that of the *End* or, more precisely, of the "activity of the end" (*SL*, 745–54). It is then the *Concept* in its free existence that is, by itself, the sublating activity. That ultimate determination of the Concept (for, beyond, it passes over into the Idea) is, moreover, accompanied by a sort of manifestation or empirical apodicticity [*apodicticité*]: in the "teleology" of the *Encyclopedia* (Remark § 204) Hegel declares that any activity (or feeling) of animal want and of appetite [*Trieb*] is one of the "readiest instances" of the teleological concept and proves that the finite is not immutable in its insurmountable difference.—The *aufheben* might then let itself quickly be identified (as in the simplest species of *Naturphilosophie*) with the finality of an appetite (the fruit *aufhebt* the germ . . .) if the end were precisely not what "requires [*erfordet*] a speculative interpretation [*auffassen*]" (*Enc. I*, § 204:280) and did not send us back in this way to the *aufheben* instead of identifying it.—Here, as elsewhere, the *aufheben* can be grasped only speculatively, that is, through the *aufheben* of the terms, the concepts, and the propositions that present it.

22. Insofar as the functioning of the text as we tried to analyze it is concerned, it might be useful to recall that there is nothing new here. Pfaff, in 1812, sketches the analysis of the circle of the *aufheben* in the same text: "If, in your circle, you do not have to move in a straight line (as the mathematicians), nor as the comets in a parabola, but rather as the planets, the dwelling place of Gods, in a full circle [*zurückkehrenden Figur*,

schließe ich auch daraus], it is because you need language whereas the mathematician is mute" (*Briefe von und an Hegel,* Bd. 1, *1785–1812,* edited by J. Hoffmeister [Hamburg: F. Meiner, 1952], 404 [my translation— Trans.]); Hegel's reply is lost, but in Pfaff's following letter one finds a trace of it: "You have drawn attention to the way in which the ground [*Grund*] lies in the thing that has already been there, and that one was only using another word [*ein anderes Wort*]" (ibid., 406 [my translation— Trans.]). In a certain way we are only attempting to comment on Hegel's other "mot," the word that does not replace a first one but the "thing" that was already (before words?) there (among words?).

23. But in fact—we should add—what is the status of this most vo- luminous part of Hegel's "work": manuals destined to be commented on, to be accompanied with Remarks (*Philosophische Propädeutik* [*Philo- sophical Propaedeutic*]; *Enzyklopädie der philosophischen Wissenschaften* [Hamburg: F. Meiner, 1992] [*Encyclopedia*]; *Grundlinien der Philosophie des Rechts,* Bd. 7 [Stuttgart: Frommann, 1964] [*Elements of the Philosophy of Right*]); and notes for the lectures, published after Hegel's death, to be accompanied with students' notes (*Vorlesungen über die Philosophie der Weltgeschichte* [Hamburg: F. Meiner, 1955] [*Lectures on the Philosophy of World History*]; *Vorlesungen über die Philosophie der Religion,* Bd. 15–17 [Stuttgart: Frommann, 1959] [*Lectures on the Philosophy of Religion*]; *Aesthetik* [Frankfurt am Main: Surhkamp, 1970] [*Aesthetics: Lectures on Fine Art*]). Where does the text end, and where do the remarks begin?— Still how does Hegel consider the Remarks that he publishes? As "exo- teric" complements, as he writes in the 1827 preface to the *Encyclopedia,* or as the genuine developments and clarification of the "more abstract parts of the text [*abstraktere Inhalt des Textes*]" (1), which consequently de- prives the book of the character of an ordinary "compendium," as the preface to the *Elements of the Philosophy of Right* notes?

24. *Lectures on the Philosophy of Religion, Together with a Work on "The Proofs of the Existence of God,"* translated by E. B. Speirs and B. Sanderson (London: Kegan Paul Trench Trübner, 1895), 3:168.

Chapter 3

1. The German text reads: "Für das spekulative Denken ist es er-

freulich, in der Sprache Wörter zu finden, welche eine spekulative Bedeutung *an ihnen selbst* haben" [my emphasis]. See Chap. 2 note 1.—Trans.

2. Ibid. What is at issue is a "word"—*dictum*—of which one of Cicero's correspondents reports that it has been attributed to him so as to do him a disservice with Octave: "laudandum adulescentem, ornandum, tollendum," where *tollendum* can mean both "to elevate" (to raise in rank) and "to push aside" or "to suppress"—cf. *Ad familiares*, XI, 20.

3. The allusion to Descartes is not so remote as it may appear. Indeed, here is an opportunity, among many others in this work, to indicate that one should reread—mutatis mutandis—the following passage from *Règles pour la direction de l'esprit* [*Rules for the Direction of the Mind*]:

In case anyone should be troubled by my novel use of the term [*vox*] *intuition* and of other terms to which I shall be forced to give a different meaning [*removere*] from their ordinary one, I wish to point out here that I am paying no attention to the way these terms have lately been used [*usurpata vocabula*] in the Schools. For it would be very difficult for me to employ the same terminology, when my own views are profoundly different. I shall take account only of the meanings in Latin of individual words and, when appropriate [*propria*] words are lacking, I shall use what seem the most suitable words, adapting them to my own meaning [*transfero ad meum sensum*]. (*Oeuvres philosophiques I*, edited by F. Alquié [Paris: Dunod, 1997], translated by J. Cottingham, R. Stoothoff, and D. Murdoch as *The Philosophical Writings of Descartes* [Cambridge: Cambridge University Press, 1985], 1:14).

Once the differences and the analogies with Hegel's text are analyzed, one might be led to other texts by other philosophers, across a chain illustrating philosophy's constant recourse to some extra word, the continual burdening of its concept with a word, or the burdening of language with unheard-of meaning—an excess of meaning that is the condition of meaning, as we know, but also an excess of words that is the condition of a text.

4. "It is the form of simple judgement, when it is used to express speculative results, which is very often responsible for the paradoxical and bizarre light in which much of recent philosophy appears to those who are not familiar with speculative thought" (*SL*, 91). The phrase "in the

trust of, in the confidence of" is a translation of "en confiance avec, dans la confidence de," Nancy's gloss of *Vertraut*. Following strictly the English translation, the sentence would read ". . . to those who are not, as Hegel wrote a few pages earlier, familiar with speculative thought."—Trans.

5. *SL*, 107.

6. *PS*, 68.

7. The statement "*Aufheben* is the *right* word" should also be heard as "*Aufheben* . . . is the *bon mot* of speculative discourse."—Trans.

8. It is worth noting that Hegel's "position" may, in fact, not be un-related to that of Socrates (Plato) in the *Cratylus*, if one follows Gérard Genette's reading of this dialogue in "L'éponymie du nom," *Critique* 28 (1972), at least insofar as Hegel, no more than Socrates, believes in a "cor-rectness of names," whether it be *thesei* or *phusei*. Simply, if according to Socrates, the *onomaturge* may have been mistaken, according to Hegel and as if through an inversion of the frequency of cases, it sometimes hap-pens that language succeeds. For the one and the other what is at issue is not the truth of words but that of a certain usage, of the play of discourse's ability to turn language to best account [*du meilleur parti à tirer de la langue au jeu du discours*]—even if this play be in turn that of truth.

9. *Lectures on the Philosophy of Religion*, 3:366. [Cf. Nancy's gloss of this passage in *Hegel, L'inquiétude du négatif*, 146 n. 29: "Let us add that for Hegel this sentence also means that philosophy reveals, or let the fol-lowing be revealed: that the 'revelation' of the triple monotheism of the West has nothing else to reveal but *this*—and thus pass over into thought, for which nothing, no more god remains at the bottom, at the surface of the absolute."—Trans.]

10. As is the rule in such cases, the second preface is devoted to the re-vision of the *Science of Logic* and therefore to the presentation rather than to the content, that is to say, in particular, to the "plasticity" that it mentions later. It concludes, or remains incomplete, with the necessity of revising a modern work "seventy-seven times," and it takes its initial theme from the insufficiency of the materials handed over by tradition, from the "disordered heap of dead bones" that the "familiar forms of thoughts" are (*SL*, 31). If the first preface introduced the *treatise*, this one prefaces the language and the style of the *book*.

11. As regards "mother tongues," we shall see later how Hegel himself obliges us to nuance or to complicate this affirmation.

12. *Reason in History: A General Introduction to the Philosophy of History*, translated by R. S. Hartman (New York: Macmillan, 1987), 75.

13. *Lectures on the History of Philosophy*, translated by E. S. Haldane (Lincoln: University of Nebraska Press, 1995), 2:34.

14. *Elements of the Philosophy of Right*, translated by T. M. Knox (Oxford: Clarendon, 1952), § 151:108.

15. *Lectures on the Philosophy of Religion*, 3:266.

16. Ibid., 322.

17. Ibid., 186.

18. *Lectures on the Philosophy of History. Introduction: Reason in History*, translated by H. B. Nisbet (Cambridge: Cambridge University Press, 1986), 51.

19. *Natural Law*, translated by T. M. Knox (Philadelphia: University of Pennsylvania Press, 1975), 91.

20. J. Derrida, "Qual Quelle" in *Marges de la philosophie* (Paris: Minuit, 1972), translated by A. Bass as *Margins of Philosophy* (Brighton: Harvester Press, 1982), 284–85. (Let us note, with respect to this example and many others, that this genre of *rapprochement* by assonance is a current practice of German, a practice that gives rise to numerous expressions and proverbs.)

21. *SL*, 45. What is at issue this time is the introduction. Let us recall, moreover, that in the epigraph of this work, a short sentence from the *Aesthetics* alone makes the three pairs of words correspond and that all this could be titled the Hegelian play around *Eigensinn*, as a capricious property.

22. One would need to emphasize and to complicate accordingly Hegel's *socratylism* (to use Genette's word) of which we spoke: it is only with respect to this chance of names [*ce hasard des noms*] that the chance of a good speculative nomination occurs.

23. "Aphorismen aus Hegels Wastebook, 1803–1806," in *Jenaer Schriften 1801–1807* (Frankfurt: Suhrkamp Verlag, 1970), 557 [my translation—Trans.].

24. Koyré had well indicated this: more particularly, let us recall that,

according to the latter, there is no Hegelian etymolog*ism* (etymology as such is empirical: [cf. in Chap. 5 the text from § 33 of *Logic*, which we are quoting]) and that, if Hegel pours out the treasure of German, he does not capitalize it in the manner of Fichte, Schelling, Humboldt, Baader, or Schleiermacher, from whom he happily borrows. (Cf. H. Stoltenberg, *Deustche Weisheitsprache* [Lahr, 1933], 29ff). With respect, at least with the most "romantic" romanticism, Hegel systematically displaces the claims of German language to be held as absolute privilege. In a nutshell, Hegel refuses to consider German as Fichte did at the beginning of the *7th Address to the German Nation*: ". . . the Germans . . . as a people that has the right to call itself simply *the* people . . . for indeed the word '*deutsch*' in its real signification denotes what we have just said" (92). This is also why he does not consider philosophy in the same way as does Fichte, who declares: "philosophy, for it is philosophy which scientifically comprehends the eternal archetype of all spiritual life. We must designate it by the foreign name, as the Germans have shown themselves unwilling to adopt the German name that was recently suggested" (*Reden an die deutsche Nation*, edited by A. Liebert [Berlin: Deutsche Bibliothek, 1912 (translated as *Addresses to the German Nation*, edited by G. A. Kelly [New York: Harper and Row, 1968], 63)]). Let us note that before romanticism Herder is at issue: all the ideas that one often attributes to Hegel concerning thought in language, the mother tongue, etc., in brief, the simple reversal of the old hierarchy of thought and language, associated with nationalism, are developed and repeated in the texts that Hegel no doubt knew—*Abhandlung über den Ursprung der Sprache* in *Sämtliche Werke V*, 33 vols. (Hildesheim: Georg Olms Verlagsbuchhandlung, 1967), translated by J. H. Moran and A. Gode as *On the Origin of Language* (Chicago: University of Chicago Press, 1986); *Über die neuere deutsche Literatur*, in *Scriften zur Literatur I* (Berlin, Weimar: Aufbau Verlag, 1985)—but whose theses he alters or displaces. This displacement entails the necessity that its "theory" be diffracted and dispersed in its text instead of being established as a set of principles.

25. December 16, 1809. *Briefe von und an Hegel*, 250 [my translation—Trans.].

26. But since the journey did not take place, one can also, in passing,

dream about Hegel's being *disappropriated*, in Dutch, of his science . . .
or else, out of malice, regret that he was not invited to China.

27. Let us note the ambiguity of the "in it" [*en elle, in ihr*], which logically refers us back to a mother tongue that the text does not name and
grammatically to "philosophy"—as if the two were confounded but also
as if the discourse were becoming embarrassed. [The ambiguity is absent
from the English text since *in ihr* is translated as "in the philosophical
realm," whereas in French ". . . welche jedoch durch den Gebrauch be-
reits das Bürgerrecht in ihr erhalten haben" is translated as ". . . mais ces
mots ont déjà reçu droit de cité en elle."—Trans.]

28. This is at least how we can understand this indecisive sentence. We
can also suppose that the "as here" recalls the case of the *aufheben*, but it
does so by implicitly distinguishing it from the cases where language
possesses an expression deprived of reflexivity. One need only ascribe to
Hegel a certain slackening of syntax and of style—many other examples
of which, incidentally, it would be possible to find in his texts.—As far as
this passage is concerned, let us in any case note that its somewhat confused logic also stems materially from the play of two editions: the first
part of the sentence—up until "Latin terms"—appears in the first edition;
in the second it is preceded by a mechanical explanation of the moment
and followed by the added ending of the sentence. Hegel seems to have
hastily sewn his additions without sufficiently supervising the overall exposition. But what does a lack of supervision on Hegel's part mean? Its
trace is in any case what is given us to read. [This note partly relies on the
fact that *cas* can denote an "occurrence," as in the phrase "comme c'est ici
le cas" (the *as here* of the English translation), and, in grammar, can point
to inflected forms of nouns, adjectives, or pronouns.—Trans.]

29. Cf. *Enc. II*, Remark § 204.

30. This passage calls for this additional commentary: by introducing
the *philosophische Kunstsprache,* Hegel evokes the language of the others,
of the philosophers who make of philosophy a technique, of the thinkers
of the understanding [*penseurs d'entendement*], if one dare say so, *and* a
language he will himself be obliged to speak from time to time in the
Science of Logic. One must thus understand that speculative philosophy,
even though it is entirely other than philosophies [*bien qu'elle soit tout*

autre que les philosophies] and is alone in thinking and in sublating, cannot hold a pure speculative discourse; it is obliged to introduce, but as if only furtively, borrowings whose origin it challenges. The exposition of the concept will not be without mixture. Mixture is not the *aufheben* but is rather the (nondialectical) opposite of it, its caricature or its counterfeiting.

31. Let us note that in the second edition, where this sentence is added, Hegel also added in brackets, at the beginning of the Remark, the ideal [*das Ideelle*] in order to render the sublated more precise—and that it is therefore the theory of the lever that, in this case, renders the discourse of the *aufheben* more precise. As far as *ideell* is concerned, let us leave aside the necessary analysis of its difference from *ideal* by simply recalling that the "ideal being [*idéel, das Ideelle*] is the finite as it is in the true infinite," that is, the determination preserved as a moment, and that the "ideal" [*das Ideale*] "has a more precise meaning (of the beautiful and of its associations)" (*SL*, 149–50). What distinguishes the two words is a nuance, a play of shadows: *Schattierung*, to which we shall come back.

32. It is rather this last hypothesis that the passage from the *Encyclopedia* to which Hegel refers in the Remark indicates:

The *transition of ideality into reality* is explicitly [*auf ausdrückliche Weise*] demonstrated in the familiar mechanical phenomena, namely, that ideality can take the place of reality, and vice versa; and only notionless thinking of the imagination and the Understanding are to blame if the identity of both is not inferred from their interchangeability. In connection with the *lever*, for instance, *distance* can take the place of *mass*, and vice versa, and a quantum of ideal moment produces the same effect as the corresponding real amount. (*Enc. II*, § 261).

The *aufheben* appears to be a property of the lever and vice versa.

33. Which amounts to saying that there is no gnosis in Hegel—if one compares his work with the lexical and literal speculations of the Gnosis (that of Marcos, for example, or of the *Pistis Sophia*) and with all the latent (or patent) German gnosticism. We could demonstrate this, notwithstanding Hegel's numerous recourse to the Word of God, to the Johannine Logos, etc., since all these recourses are as many *sublations* of

religious representations. Failing to be able here to dwell on this other process, let us at least signal the Hegelian critique of "superstition of the understanding" toward certain words, such as, for example, "*infinite*" (*SL*, 301).

Chapter 4

1. Hegel, "Aphorismen aus Hegels Wastebook, 1803–1806." Translated as "Aphorism from the Wastebook," *Independent Journal of Philosophy* 3 (1979): 4.

2. Ibid. *Proposition* is *Satz*, but, as in French, it is as much the syntactical unity as the theoretical or axiomatic *principle*, or still the *thesis*. Everything that follows should be considered with respect to these joint acceptations.—Let us also note that we are leaving aside Hegel's ambiguous effort to separate, in some texts, the *Satz* from judgment (*Urteil*), following traditional logic and Kant. The *Satz* always remains essentially the form of the *urteilen* proper, that is, of the determining and differentiating operation, through which the concept leaves its abstraction and begins to become (the thing).

3. Annulation: the formation of rings or ringlike divisions; a ringlike structure (OED). On the motif of the *anneau* in relation to the hermeneutic circle, see *Le partage des voix* (Paris: Galilée, 1982), 61ff.—Trans.

4. What follows refers us back constantly and globally to the chapters on judgment and on the syllogism in the *Science of Logic* and in the *Encyclopedia*, without it being necessary to recall all their steps and their theses.

5. In a general way one could draw many lessons from the comparative study of the various moments of the *aufheben* in a Hegelian process (that of the *Science of Logic*, the *Phenomenology*, etc.) or from one process to the other. For the operation is perhaps never quite the same in each of these episodes of sublation; the accent is put on one *moment* or the other, just as on suppression or on preservation—as if the *aufheben* in act ceaselessly oscillated on each side of its concept.

6. This word is also, for example, the one Hegel uses to characterize the role of the works of ancient culture, which one must study in order to make up for the lacks of our modern culture—according to a dialectic

that is also that of making up for the defects that the thoughtless use of our language entails—through the study of an ancient language (cf. the School Address that we quote later).

7. The adverb *schlechthin* ["purement et simplement"], which Nancy underlines, does not appear in the existing English translation. See Chap. 2.—Trans.

8. The rest of the text goes along these lines: concerning the speculative, Hegel requests that one should not forget to state the two opposite propositions. Nothing is, for all that, *decided*. . . .

9. *Encyclopédie des sciences philosophiques: La science de la logique*, translated by B. Bourgeois (Paris: Vrin, 1970), 427. The French translation quoted by Nancy reads, "Cette opération, écrit Hegel, 's'est réalisée tout d'abord à même la forme'" (*RS*, 110).—Trans.

10. One cannot fail to note that this *an* forms one of the syntactic and semantic elements of the dialectical process in general, through the expression *an sich*—too often unfortunately translated as "within, into, in oneself" [*en soi*], whereas *in sich* is also used in Hegel. In a certain way the aseity and the ipseity of the Hegelian Self [*Selbst*] are undoubtedly also played out on the side of this preposition.

11. Generally speaking, language [*la langue et le langage*] is always subtilized [*subtilisé*] in Hegel's discourse. Thus, in the *Science of Logic*, as we have already noted, the whole of the logic of the logical (speculative) expression is won in particular by means of a subtilization of natural language against all forms of symbolization, notably of mathematical symbolization (it is one of the constants of the logic proper to the Remarks); in these conditions it is possible to appreciate the (calculated?) subtlety of the movement that has to present language:

It is therefore quite inappropriate [*unpassend*] for the purpose of grasping [*fassen*] such an inner totality, to seek to apply numerical and spatial relationships in which all determinations fall asunder; on the contrary, they are the last and worst medium which could be employed. Natural relationships such as magnetism, or colour relations, would be infinitely higher and truer symbols for the purpose. Since man has in language [*die Sprache*] a means of designation peculiar to Reason [*das eigentümliche Bezeichnung-mittel*], it is an idle fancy [*ein müssiger Einfall*] to search for a less perfect mode of representation [*Darstellungsweise*] to plague oneself with. It is essentially only spirit that can comprehend the Concept as Concept; for this is not merely the property of spirit but spirit's pure self. It is futile to seek to fix it [*festhalten*] by spatial figures and algebraic signs for the purpose of the *outer eye* and an *uncomprehending mode of treatment* [Behandlungsweise] such as *calculus*. In fact, anything else which might be supposed to serve as a symbol can at most, like symbols for the nature of God, evoke imitations and echoes of the Concept. (*SL*, 618)

And so continues Hegel's argument until the end of this Remark, which does nothing other than critique the use of symbols. Language has here barely been posited; it is subtilized—conjured away and evaporated and/or made as subtle as the "spirit." But it has not gone somewhere else or beyond. It looks as though it were being evaporated in itself, in the self-evidence of its determinate being [*être-là*], *an der Form*. And if the sub-tilization is alchemical, there is here, however, no "alchemy of the verb"; language is subtilized in the *medium* that it is. It is true that language as *medium* is the analogue of water in chemistry (ibid., 729); water is the neutral of the exchange, of the mixture and the passage, the dissolution of determinations (we will come back to this later); and "the neutral first water in which everything is contained, but not yet separated out" (*Enc. I*, Addition § 206:283), is Thalès's "speculative water," a "speculative water" that is not a metaphor, a declared or genuine turn of language [*un tour avoué ou avéré de langage*], but is, with far more subtlety, *matter*, "devoid of form" and without "a sensuous universality" (ibid.). Each time language is "at issue," a formless matter is inscribed right at the level of form—or conversely, the form of the concept is written on water.

12. See, for example, *Glauben und Wissen* (Leipzig: F. Meiner, 1928), translated by Walter Cerf and H. S. Harris as *Faith and Knowledge* (Albany: State University of New York Press, 1977).

13. September 29, 1809, in *Hegels sämtliche Werke*, Bd. 3, Jubiläum-Ausgabe, edited by H. Glockner (Stuttgart: Fromann, 1961).

14. Ibid., 242 [my translation—Trans.].

15. One must relate the analysis of a few other texts to this singular, irresolute position of grammar. Consider, for example, the introduction to the *Science of Logic*, where Hegel develops a double *discourse*, whose logic is disconcerting: (1) he *compares* logic to grammar, as two routes leading from abstraction to the wealth of spirit ("he who has mastered a lan-

guage and at the same time has a comparative knowledge of other languages, he alone can make contact with the spirit and culture of a people through the grammar of its language" [57–58]); (2) but, in the midst of the parallel, one discovers that the final wealth of grammatical culture leads to logic itself ("through the grammar [*durch die Grammatik hindurch*] he can recognize the expression of mind as such, that is, logic" [57]. Let us note the "*durch . . . hindurch*": *durch* alone means "by means of" — *durch-hindurch* means "passing through," which implies that one disappears into it, as into the woods, and that one comes through it, as light through a transparent body). Nothing later comes to resolve this mixture of comparison and consequence.—But consider also these texts concerning the fact that Indian grammar—or more widely the grammars of "primitive" people—are more developed than modern grammars, a development that clashes with those of the other elements of culture and acts against the logic of history. This fact is transformed into the confusion of the thinker. Hegel evokes it in the Remark of the *Encyclopedia* that we just quoted and in the *Philosophy of History* on the Indians, primitive peoples who have remained "voiceless and dumb," without written history:

> It is a fact [*Faktum*] revealed by philological monuments, that languages, during a rude condition of the nations that have spoken them, have been very highly developed; that the human understanding occupied this theoretical region with great ingenuity and completeness. For Grammar, in its extended and consistent form, is the work of thought, which makes its categories distinctly visible [*bemerklich macht*] therein. It is moreover, a fact, that with advancing social and political civilization, this systematic completeness of intelligence suffers attrition . . . : a singular phenomenon [*eigentümliches Phänomen*]—that the progress towards a more highly intellectual condition, while expanding and cultivating rationality, should disregard that intelligent amplitude and expressiveness—should find it an obstruction and contrive to do without it. (*Philosophy of History*, translated by J. Sibree [New York: Dover, 1956], 62–63)

Remarkable, strange (*eigentümlich*: proper, singular, and abandoned), grammar is outdone in the progress of the spirit. But one should therefore ask what remains, in the wealth of a modern language (and in the poorness of its grammar), of this lost development—for example, these remnants of etymology that Hegel, without consistent etymologizing, scatters in his texts. These remnants are not, in any case, of prodigal origin; they are rather remnants of remnants, remnants of an outgrowth or an aberration of barbarian grammar.

16. Yet it is this tradition that has always sought logically to take over grammar—but, in Port-Royal itself, an irreducible difference, as small as it may be, still separates the *Grammaire générale et raisonnée* and the *Science of Logic*. Grammar as such will always be, in spite of everything, *Vaugelas'* twofold principle of *usage* and of the *analogy*, where "reason is not at all at issue," and which must be compared to faith: in both cases "we keep finding reason in things [*aux choses*] which are beyond reason" (Preface to *Remarques sur la langue française* [1690; reprint, Geneva: Slatkine, 1972]). Hegel, in this case, might be emphasizing the gap: a "grammar, in its extended and consistent form"—a formula that we read in the preceding note—is not even a "general and rational grammar."

17. School Address, September 29, 1809, *Sämtliche Werke*, Bd. 3, Jubilaüm-Ausgabe, edited by H. Glockner (Stuttgart: Fr. Fromman Verlag, 1961), 241.

18. *Enc. I*, § 193 and Remark.

19. Ibid., § 195. This subordination of mechanism, this strange nonsublated and nonsublatable slave position—although constituting a sublating machine—or this kind of indecision or of mechanical blockage of the *aufheben*, draws attention to itself in many places in Hegel. For example, at the decisive moment when teleology will ensure the passage from the object to the Idea: "This relation [purposive activity] is the sphere of mechanism and chemism which now *serve* the purpose—which is the truth and the free Concept of them both. The fact that the subjective purpose, as the power over these processes (in which the *objective* gets used up [*abreibt*] through mutual friction and sublates itself), keeps itself *outside of them* and *preserves itself* in them is the *cunning* of reason" (*Enc. I*, § 209:284). Thus: (1) the *aufheben* of the object is determined (or in any case is contaminated) by mere use [*usure*]; (2) the subjective is preserved, protected from wear and usury and from the *aufheben*, beyond the reach of the cogwheels of the machine; (3) the most important thing is the cunning of reason, which is manifest, as we see, above all as the cunning of Hegel's text, which here spares the *subject* the ultimate mechanical rigors

of the *aufheben*. To speculate well one must indeed know how to use this "right" word (this bon mot) advisedly, skillfully. . . .

20. They should not be confused with the unique syllable equivalent to nothing—"Om, Om, Om"—which the Brahma, "dull, empty consciousness," "says inwardly" (*SL*, 97). It is not an inner voice that speaks in these words. Is it still a voice? Yes, but on condition that one unfolds carefully its *supplementary* structure: cf. J. Derrida, *La voix et le phénomène: Introduction au problème du signe dans la phénoménologie de Husserl* (Paris: P.U.F., 1972), translated by D. B. Allison as *Speech and Phenomena and Other Essays on Husserl's Theory of the Sign*, (Evanston: Northwestern University Press, 1973), chap. 7. Does recitation not lead us, moreover, to Jacobi's original vowel awaiting its accent? One spells out the "vowels of the spirit," but they are plural, and the situation is not an original one: one loses the accent. Instead of giving rise (giving birth) to a language, one undoes or disconcerts a language.

21. This metrics is preceded or accompanied by another form, more literal or less literary, of a mechanics of the proposition: that of the "counterthrust," of the Predicate as "an independent mass" and as the "weight" that "impedes" thinking, in the paragraph preceding the one we quote (*PS*, 37).

22. Comte de Lautréamont, *Les chants de Maldoror* in *Oeuvres complètes* (Paris: Corti, 1963), translated by P. Knight as *Maldoror* and *Poems* (Harmondsworth, Middlesex, England: Penguin, 1978), 42.

Chapter 5

1. That *relief* and *sublation* be doublets is the case when *Aufhebung* is translated as *relève*. *Relief* and *relever* are both derived from the Latin *relevare* (*relever*).—Trans.

2. There is no English equivalent to the verb *virguler*, which means "ponctuer en marquant les virgules" or figuratively "marquer de petits traits en forme de virgule" (*Petit Robert*).—Trans.

3. We can thus distinguish more clearly what we tried to put forward above: this speculative abyss [*abyme*] might constitute the optical and the specular abyss within itself, that of the infinite play of reflections—and the abyss [*abyme*] or the heraldic abyss [*abîme*]. The latter, at the heart of the

coat of arms, between its flanks, its points and its canton, above its navel, is the necessary position of the piece or of the figure when it is unique (it is then said to be "en abîme"). In this case—in fact, rare—it often happens that the figure repeats the color (or the metal or the fur) of another part of the blason—a disjointed repetition that allows us to see and to blazon (to decipher, to "describe in proper heraldic language" [OED] or, in the figurative sense of the verb, to parody or to speak ill of somebody). Redoubling very closely the philosophical optic, this heraldics would appear constantly to have to read a relief in the abyss [*à lire un relief dans l'abîme*], a gap or a reef in the identification of the Absolute.

4. Immediately before, the "other" modes, which are related to the "particular philosophical sciences," have been signposted by Hegel under at least the recognized species of *art* and *religion*. What the one (and) the other have to do with the style of the *aufheben* should be examined elsewhere.

5. As we pointed out, primitive, barbarous languages were less poor, less worn out. But this originary oddness—which, in any case, might not even be that of *a* language—is as neglected by philosophical history as it passes unnoticed in speculative words. The latter, with their wealth, are at the most the remainders of an origin that is itself outdone, a dismembered origin, half-consumed and then abandoned in the course of the dispersions and the migrations of barbarous peoples (*Philosophy of History*) and upon which one sometimes comes in passing, while speaking,—*what is it?* Can one even ask?

6. It thus comes back into the orb. But the Hegelian particularity would then be that the orb is made or is marked by reliefs. There is no "Copernican revolution" in Hegel—there might instead be a distortion of the orbs or any other accident that might disturb its purity. Should one therefore compare Hegel to what he was himself proposing as a critical image of Jacobi's philosophy: "Attached to the ring, which it offers as a symbol of Reason, there is a piece of the skin from the hand that offers it; and if Reason is scientific connection, and has to do with concepts, we can very well do without that piece of skin" (*Faith and Knowledge*, translated by W. Cerf and H. S. Harris [Albany: State University of New York Press, 1977], 117)? Or should one question the very choice or the fabrica-

tion of such a disquieting image—among few others in fact—in Hegel's text, and, hence, interrogate another form of exorbitance. We will have the opportunity to deal with these questions elsewhere.

7. As elsewhere throughout the book, "a good word" also reads as "a bon mot."—Trans.

8. Ibid.—The rest of the paragraph adds that the preceding moments have been syntheses of the same elements but that creative imagination is no longer a synthesis, an extrinsic reunion, but "concrete subjectivity."—Let us note in passing the following: everyone knows that this theory of imagination probably represents the point where one can say that Hegel is the closest to Kant (as J. Derrida notes in "The Pit and the Pyramid" [79]) and where, if you like, in the Hegelian *aufheben* of Kant, the *bewahren* wins over the *aufhören lassen*. Now, it is at this point in Kant that the *Bedeutung* of the *Begriff* occurs through the *Schema*; we will show elsewhere (*The analogical discourse of Kant*) that the schema has the singular course ("monogrammatic") and the singular status ("indirect," figurative, rhetorical, *witzig*, "sublime," and even monstrous) that determine the philosophical *Exhibition* as that which remains withdrawn from an impossible *Darstellung* and that dooms the *Bedeutung* to function only as its "own" analogy. In this respect, then, the insistence of a Kantian moment or motif in Hegel could well also be, in the very process of the *spekulative Bedeutung*, the resistance of a foreign body to its *aufheben*. Like the machine, Kant might remain *inassimilable*.

9. Cf. *Enc. III*, § 445.

10. "Being-found" is the English translation of "être-trouvé," which renders *Gefundensein*. See the passage from the *Encyclopedia* quoted above, where *Gefundensein* is translated as "what is picked up."—Trans.

11. Cf. *A*, 1:304.

12. *Enc. I*, § 33:70.

In its orderly shape this metaphysics had, as its *first part*, Ontology, the doctrine of *abstract determinations of essence*. In their manifoldness and finite validity, these determinations lack a principle; they must therefore be enumerated *empirically* and *contingently*, and their more precise *content* can only be based upon representation, [i.e.,] based upon the assurance that by one word one thinks precisely this, or perhaps also upon the word's etymology. What can be at issue in this context is merely the correctness of the analysis as it corresponds with the usage of language, and the empirical *exhaustiveness*, not the *truth* and *necessity* of these determinations in and for themselves.

There are thus—as we shall see—many (dogmatic or speculative) ways to "correspond" to the usage of language.

13. The difference at issue is that of representation, but which one exactly? All the more so since *von ihrem Unterschiede* could almost be translated as "float on the basis of its difference"—conceptual and syntactical confusions are here at least possible. [It might be useful to refer to the German passage: "Es muß daher genügen, wenn der Vorstellung bei ihren Ausdrücken, die für philosophische Bestimmungen gebraucht werden, so etwas Ungefähres von ihrem Unterschiede vorschwebt, wie es bei jenen Ausdrücken der Fall sein mag, daß man in ihnen Schattierungen der Vorstellung erkennt, welche sich näher auf die entsprechenden" (*Wissenschaft der Logik*, 357–58).—Trans.]

14. In maritime law the wreckage belongs to the one who finds it and who is called the inventor. In general Right, what is lost and without owner is a "wreckage." That the ownership of the salvage fall to the State will not strike a good Hegelian. . . .

15. *Work* renders "qui *fait marcher*," which echoes the *jemandem etwas vorschweben* (to pull someone's leg) of the passage quoted above and can also mean to make the text or the reader progress.—Trans.

16. Cf. *A*, 1:304–5. *Zweifelhaftigkeit* is the ambiguity, the equivocation that provokes doubt—which leaves one pensive or wavering. *Doppelsinnigkeit* is the twofold meaning, the straightforward polysemy—it is the lexical stage. Hegel also uses *Zweideutigkeit*, which is closer to the second of these terms, for the "meaning" of the first. Between *Doppelsinnigkeit* and *Zweideutigkeit*, there is only a *Schattierung*.

17. Cf. *A*, 1:306, the lion of heroic strength.

18. Ibid., 404.—Hegel does here more than to come near Kant. He repeats the text of the "indirect hypotyposis" or the "symbolic" of § 59 of the *Third Critique* (see *Kritik der Urteilskraft*, edited by K. Vorlander [Leipzig: F. Meiner, 1922]). This is not without importance, obviously, for

the analysis of a Kantian resistance in the Hegelian *aufheben*, which is noted above.

19. Immediately after, Hegel states that etymology is incapable of allowing us to know exactly what is literal and what is metaphorical in a dead language.

20. *A*, 1:406. This rather rare term does not seem to have a strict lexical use in Hegel. Here, it can only be the matter of an "enunciation" connoting the poetical [*le poétique*]. It occurs after the few pages where the expressions "*metaphorische Ausdruck*" and "*das Metaphorische*" have been used and above all where the poetical metaphor, that of the *Dichtung*, has been evoked, which, in its primary sense, is a "dictation."

21. *PS*, 493. The quotation is in fact inexact: "From the chalice of this realm of spirits foams forth for Him his own infinitude"; this is the lot of recitation.

22. Cf. the Addition to § 82:132 of the *Encyclopedia*:

The term *speculation* tends to be used in ordinary life in a very vague, and at the same time, secondary sense—as, for instance, when people talk about a matrimonial or commercial speculation. All that it is taken to mean here is that, on the one hand, what is immediately present must be transcended, and, on the other, that whatever the content of these speculations may be, although it is initially only something subjective, it ought not to remain so, but is to be realized or translated into objectivity.

One could add (or confront) the following, from a letter from Pfaff in 1812. After having written, "It is peculiar that *Germans* do not have a second word for *abstracting* or for *reflecting*. The first one is borrowed from mechanics, the second from optics"; he writes, "Speculative thought. Once again a *Latin* word borrowed from *optics* (could you please indicate to me the Greek expressions). *Speculation* comes from *speculum*, mirror, the thought that gazes at itself (that is reflected) . . ." (*Briefe von und an Hegel*, 407–8). Hegel's answer, if ever there was one, is lost.

23. Of course, this madness outside words [*hors-les-mots*] "recalls" Hegel's avowal of his fear to become mad, as Georges Bataille has—not so much picked out [*relevé*] as written—and that Derrida has noticed [*remarqué*] in Bataille (cf. "From Restricted to General Economy," 251–77).

24. Must we not, indeed, reconsider from this point the long struggle Hegel has taken up against the "ineffable" and the "philosophy of feeling" (a struggle continually taken up again since *Faith and Knowledge* and through all the texts). The *reason* that is struggling here (and that simultaneously challenges understanding) does not affirm the positive rights of a rationality; it defends itself against the madness that it itself is; it averts its innermost and its most intimate threat, that of an "outside meaning" [*hors-sens*] alongside which, right at the side of which [*à même*], continuously, perilously, speculative meaning is won over. But it cannot be won over without causing the mad face of its double to appear in the *speculum*. *Aufheben* is to avert this mirror, to guarantee the success of this ordeal; but the discourse of the *aufheben* ceaselessly renews the threat (ceaselessly threatens itself) [*ne cesse de (se) renouveler la menace*].

25. *Enc. III*, Addition § 462:221. Let us note the sort of *Schattierung* that plays, in this text, between the *thing* (*Sache*, the matter, the content, the *Thing itself*) and *something* (*etwas*, the indeterminate, the outside), which makes the one slip or fall over the other. [The nuance at issue around *etwas* is hard to perceive in the English translation: *etwas* is left out of at least one of the sentences that Nancy underlines in the French translation of "zu etwas ganz leerem" as "devient quelque chose (*etwas*) de tout à fait vide." In English one has: "becomes quite empty."—Trans.]

26. But the middle (the means or the middle) [*le moyen ou le milieu*]— by means of which and through which any syllogism and any *aufheben* occurs—is essentially broken [*die gebrochene Mitte*]. One only has to refer to the sections on the syllogism and on the object in the *Science of Logic* and in the *Encyclopedia*.

27. Quite a complex gesture, since Socrates (as we recalled in the preamble) is a "plastic nature" one cannot imagine being able to find "today"—lost, in relief in history (with the dialogue involving plastic characters and a little like the "barbarous" grammar); but it is also the bearer of a still abstract universality toward which one must share Aristophanes' irony (*LHP*, 1:402). He is also the one in whom the "subjectivity of thought" has deepened to the point of manifesting itself outwardly: "once, sunk in a deep meditation, he stood immovable on one spot the whole day and night. . . . This was a cataleptic state, which may

bear some relation to magnetic somnambulism, in which Socrates became quite dead to sensuous consciousness" (ibid., 390–91).

28. What follows concerning the *Witz* will remain succinct insofar as we will devote ulterior studies to Hegel and to other authors (the beginning of which can be found in the presentation of Jean-Paul's *Sur le Witz* in *Poétique*, n. 15). Let us indicate that one should above all add to what we will evoke here concerning the complexity of the *Witz* in the Hegelian system, the complexity of the relations that the *History of Philosophy* entertains with the comic and the *Witz* in this history: Aristophanes, Eubulides, Stilpo, Aristippus, the Cynics, etc. And let us add, since it relates to previous notes, that the *Witz* occupies a singularly different place in Kant. But one should moreover briefly explain an absence: that of Freud, whose role might be unavoidable. It is only too obvious that this reading could only take place after Freud. On the other hand, it would probably have been too easily seductive to seek to master Hegel's text on the basis of the Freudian *Witz*. This would have amounted to granting Freud the function of a dialectical, speculative, Hegelian truth, to delegate to him the vigilance that Hegel failed to have. . . . One will begin to be able to discern Freud's "role" only once such a function will have been carefully pushed aside. The reading of Hegel can help us in this, a reading that, for this reason, we hoped to hold "by a word" to Freud.

29. Thus a history comparable to that of grammar.

30. Ibid., 489. Let us note, with this word and many others that, as we saw, accompany and qualify the *Witz*, the abundance of French terms used by Hegel as a case in point. It is as if, concerning the *Witz*, one had to write in the language of the "spiritual" nation and, as a result, in a foreign language.

31. "Hamanns Schriften," in *Hegels sämtliche Werke*, Bd. 20, Jubiläum-Ausgabe, edited by H. Glockner (Stuttgart: Fromann, 1958), 252.

32. Ibid., 253.

Chapter 6

1. This does not mean that the "concept," the motif (indeed, the mobile), or the word *text* functions, where it functions, on an identical mode to that of Hegel's "empty word," but neither does it mean that it functions

on a mode *simply* external or opposed to the latter. It is what we hope to have shown here concerning both these points—here where, incidentally, we are undertaking neither a thematics nor a systematics of the text for two reasons. First, because we wanted to devote and to limit ourselves to the conditions of reading of Hegel's text in as literal a sense as possible. The literality of a philosophical text is what traditionally has always gone without saying, to the point of being left in the shadow of the concept. Consequently, that it should be persecuted and put right in order to extract the spirit from it has always gone without saying. We will here have seen how Hegelian literality *goes without saying*, as far as it is concerned. . . .—Second, because, in spite of overzealous accommodations or narrow-minded accusations, there is no *theory* (doctrine, science, truth, discourse) of the "text" if, at least with respect to philosophy, this word or this motif points to nothing else but the operation and the transformation to which *theory* as such, *given that it has always been conceived in conformity with a surplus over every language*, irreversibly entails. (That is to say that theory as such is unable to carry out the *annulment* that [*en tout sens et en tous sens*] constitutes its very paradigm.)—To speak of "Hegel's text," therefore, above all comes down to *not* performing on Hegel [*ne pas répéter sur Hegel*] the (assuredly Hegelian, and as a result unavoidable, at least *in a sense*) operation, which is so common, and which amounts to *conceiving* of his thought or of his doctrine (better). Still even less does it come down to the (simpler or more elusive) operation that consists of declaring it inconceivable or monstrous. On the contrary, to speak of Hegel's text amounts (very simply, but in all rigor) to letting what has been written and signed by Hegel's name to be reread—and which, *for this very reason*, and according to a few constraints of philosophy *itself*, cannot not have cut into, exceeded, or marred the property, the veracity, the logic of philosophical discourse (as happens to the stage director who has striven too hard for "realism").—To reread, to reread a philosophical text, would appear to consist of "recognizing" in it what literally does not let itself be constructed or deduced (and we shall soon see the extent to which Hegel has literally insisted on the necessity of reading), what, if one dare say so, *is lost at sight* [*à livre ouvert s'y perd*]. Since the Plato of the Theaetetus, of the Sophist, and of the Parmenides, certain losses (father, the proper, the One) might be very regularly inscribed in philosophy and of philosophy—of which the logical *aufheben* might then just as well accomplish the general sublation as the textual break-down. This counting, this calculation, and this double reading of the *aufheben* are assuredly possible only on condition that one has taken into account what, in philosophy, in our time, has raised the question as question "of" our time (as an active, practical, modifying, transforming or de-forming: a twisted and twisting question). We uttered, at the beginning, the name of Heidegger. It is time, in conclusion, to turn to a text that stands in a strange proximity—that is to say also at a strange distance—to Hegel's texts that we considered. Without the subtle but irreversible twists (even though they too are to be "reread") that the former has im-parted to the latter, nothing no doubt might have come to disturb the Hegelianism embalmed in its text:

> The meaning-fullness of language by no means consists in a mere accumu-lation of meanings cropping up haphazardly. It is based on a play which, the more richly it unfolds, the more strictly it is bound by a hidden rule. Through this, meaning-fullness plays a part in what has been selected and weighed in the scale whose oscillations we seldom experience. That is why what is said is bound by the highest law. That is the freedom which gives freedom to the all-playing structure of never-resting transformation. . . . This language is not the expression of thinking, but is thinking itself, its stride and its voice. (M. Heidegger, *The Question of Being*, translated by W. Kluback and J. T. Wilde [n.p.: Vision, 1956])

2. *Enc. II*, § 334:264. Cf. also the whole of the chemical syllogistic of the Remark of this paragraph.

3. *Lectures on the Philosophy of Religion: The Lectures of 1827*, edited by P. C. Hodgson, translated by R. F. Brown, P. C. Hodgson, and J. M. Stewart, with the assistance of H. S. Harris (Berkeley: University of California Press, 1988), 425.

4. *Lectures on the Philosophy of Religion*, 3:356.

5. The "writing," let us recall, is itself singular of all these texts: Hegel's notes are mixed up with students' notes. One can never exclude a mistake, even if one cannot also prove it. More particularly, is what is to be read in these texts not above all Hegel's mode of "writing," the small amount

of care that the professor shows for the letter of its system, abandoned to so many chances, a way of not supervising words that combine the arrogance of Thought and the restlessness of speculative thought?

6. *A*, 2:1236 (our emphasis). We are here limiting ourselves to these indications, among many others, as far as the occurrences of these terms throughout the *Aesthetics* are concerned. As one can surmise, what is also at issue is the very economy of aesthetics in Hegelian philosophy, which is probably at work in the thin interval between sublation and dissolution. There is no question of developing its analysis.—But let us not forget that the *Aesthetics* contains, in particular, the exhibition of a "marvelous" word already mentioned: *Sinn*, the double meaning of meaning [*double sens du sens*]—not to mention at the same time that the aesthetics is the domain of a plastics, the double meaning of which was indicated and taken away from us from the outset, by way of exposition. . . . —Here as elsewhere, the passage, in Hegel—or under Hegel's pen—from one book to the other, from a text to a lecture course, from chapter to remark, from one meaning to the other, and, consequently, the passage of meaning, should perhaps turn out to be like the transformation or the deformation—the modification, in the *Schreibart*—of the unique form that philosophy is: "Philosophy really has no other content" than "form alone" (*LHP*, 1:55). This purity "is," insofar as it is uttered (is proposed) and written (which the concept requires), the passage "itself"—the *aufheben*, then, that is, the difference or the differentiation of forms, the carrying along of a form (word, proposition) that goes without saying, into its other, its alteration, from *aufheben* to *auflösen* or from *Sinn* to *Sinn*. In order to have recourse to the (speculative) wealth of language, one may say that what is at issue is a continual inflection [*dé-sinence*]: a loss of meaning, a grammatical modification, a way of ending at any time. Or, provisionally, one may write: the *mise en forme* of (speculative) philosophy "is" the difference of forms, or the "being-different" of "the" form, as the being of "being" in its difference (its identity, then), or else: (speculative) philosophy (is) (the) *deformation of being*.

7. *Philosophy of History*, translated by J. Sibree (New York: Dover, 1956), 355.

8. Ibid. This note comes after the following sentence: "This impo-

tence of Nature sets limits to philosophy and it is quite improper to expect the Concept to comprehend—or as it is said, construe or deduce—these contingent products of Nature" (*Enc. II*, Remark, § 250:23). One could yet add to the note that we are about to read the following passage, where the pen (as well as the accent), since it is held by the hand that writes, was (almost) sublatable:

Thus the simple lines of the hand, the timbre and compass of the voice as the individual characteristic of speech—this too again as expressed in writing, where the hand gives it a more durable existence than the voice does, especially in the particular style of handwriting—all this is an expression of the inner, so that, as a *simple externality*, the expression again stands over against the *manifold externality* of action and fate, stands in relation to them as an *inner*. (*PS*, 189)

The "accident" at issue occurs *between the inside of the hand and the pen.*

9. *Hegel: The Letters*, translated by C. Butler and C. Seiler (Bloomington: Indiana University Press, 1984), 244.

The Speculative Unrest

1. I am very grateful to Malgorzata Kwieniewska, who, in the course of a work on this book, has tracked down the word and the motif.

2. "L'inquiétude ne nomme ni ne surnomme l'aufheben: elle l'inquiète" (*RS*, 109). See supra, Chap. 4.—Trans.

Appendix

1. Nancy, *Le discours de la syncope*, 66.

2. D. Henrich, "Hegels Theorie über den Zufall," in *Hegel im Kontext* (Frankfurt am Main: Suhrkamp, 1971), 174.

3. Cf. supra, Chap. 6 (*RS*, 176).

4. "The Thing, the thing-in-itself, the matter of thought contributes to babelize the privileged language," writes Nancy (Chap. 3, *RS*, 89), concerning Hegel's tendency to rely, in addition to the words with a double meaning in German, on those of other languages.

5. Let us note here, however, that, concerning Hegel's bons mots, Derrida speaks of an "exemplary play" that "makes possible all plays" (*Glas I* [Paris: Denoël/Gonthier, 1981], 41). But later still in *Glas* he evokes the

possibility of "demarcating the *Aufhebung* from Hegel's *vouloir-dire*" (*Glas II*, 241).

6. On the sliding of the *Aufhebung* toward the *Auflösung*, see supra, Chap. 4.

7. Koyré had explained the use of "puns" in Hegel by the fact that, for the author of the *Philosophy of History*, "unfolding [*Entwicklung*] falls in time," which means that "something," but also perhaps its opposite, and therefore the concept of the spirit "also implies contingency, the inessential of determinate being [*être-là*]" ("La terminologie hégélienne," in *Études d'histoire de la pensée philosophique* [Paris: Gallimard, 1971], 211). The becoming of history might be all the better *aufgehoben* in the untranslatable twofold meanings that have accumulated in the course of the history of a language—such as, for example, in the double meaning of the term *aufheben* itself.

8. Referring to Catherine Malabou, *L'avenir de Hegel* (Paris: Vrin, 1996), Derrida speaks of a philosophy of contingency made possible by means of the "plasticity" of language. See J. Derrida, "Le temps des adieux," *Revue philosophique* 1 (1998): 7.

9. Cf. *Duden/Etymologie* (Mannheim: Dudenverlag, 1989), 816ff.

10. Letter of April 6, 1909, *Freud/Jung, Briefwechsel* (Frankfurt am Main: S. Fisher, 1974), 243.

11. S. Freud, *Der Witz und seine Beziehung zum Unbewussten* (1905; reprint, Frankfurt am Main: Fisher Verlag, 1992), translated and edited by J. Strachey as *Jokes and Their Relation to the Unconscious*, in vol. 8 of *The Standard Edition of the Complete Psychological Works of Sigmund Freud* (London: Hogarth, 1960), 19. Further references to this text will be indicated in parentheses in the text.

12. Hegel: a philosophy not without *Witz*, defining its concept broadly but expressing an aversion for the latter; Freud: "laborious investigation" without *Witz*, defining its concept restrictively but expressing its sympathy for it.

13. Jean Baudrillard, "Le *Witz*—ou le phantasme de l'économique chez Freud," in *L'échange symbolique et la mort* (Paris: Gallimard, 1976), 328. Baudrillard speaks of an "actualisation" or of a "symbolisation," which might take place "in the sacrifice of meaning." The possibilities of

preservation of singularity in language are of course not limited to the spiritual or to the meaningless. In order to get an idea of the many facets of the problem, cf. one of Jacques Lacan's remarks on the representation of evil through the "mauvais littéraire" in Sade: "Que le livre tombe des mains prouve sans doute qu'il est mauvais, mais le mauvais littéraire est peut-être ici le garant de cette *mauvaiseté*—pour employer un terme encore en usage au XVIIIe siècle—qui est l'objet de notre recherche" (*L'éthique de la psychanalyse: Le séminaire, livre VII* [Paris: Seuil, 1986], 237). In a work titled "Passe impossible" I tried to indicate the clinical implications of such a point of view (*La lettre mensuelle* 171 [1998]: 8–14).

14. *Enc. I*, Addition § 212:286: "The good, the absolute good, fulfills itself eternally in the world, and the result is that it is already fulfilled in and for itself and does not need to wait upon us for this to happen." In a similar way, concerning adolescence [*Jünglingsalter*] (to be distinguished from adult age [*Mannesalter*]), Hegel writes in § 396 of the *Encyclopedia*: "The fact that the substantial universal contained in his ideal, in keeping with its essential nature, has already succeeded in explicating and actualizing itself, this is not perceived by the enthusiastic spirit of the youth" (61).

15. Hence, the conception developed here is in fact distinct from what Baudelaire writes on laughter: ". . . for the phenomena engendered by the fall will become the means of redemption" ("De l'essence du rire," in *Oeuvres complètes* [Paris: Gallimard, 1976], 2:528).

Cultural Memory in the Present